D1727812

SANDWICH BOOK

PUBLISHER REPRESENTATIVE OFFICE
UNITED STATES: Prime Communication System
           P.O.BOX456 Shaw Island, WA 98286
AUTHOR'S SALES AGENCY: A.K. HARANO COMPANY
           P.O. Box 1022 Edmonds, WA 98020
           Phone: (206) 774-5490
           D & BH ENTERPRISES
           94-443 Kahuanani Street, Waipahu, HI 96797
           Phone: (808) 671-6041
           LEW PUBLISHING CO.,
           7200 E.Greenlake Drive, North,
           Seattle, Washington 98115
           Phone: (206) 525-6510
           FAX: (206) 525-6970
OVERSEAS DISTRIBUTORS
UNITED STATES: JP TRADING, INC.
           300 Industrial Way
           Brisbane, Calif. 94005
           Phone: (415) 468-0775, 0776
MEXICO: Publicaciones Sayrols, S.A. de C.V.
COLOMBIA: Jorge E. Morales & CIA. LTDA.
TAIWAN: Formosan Magazine Press, Ltd.
HONG KONG: Apollo Book Company, Ltd.
THAILAND: Central Department Store Ltd.
SINGAPORE: MPH DISTRIBUTORS (S) PTE, LTD.
MALAYSIA: MPH DISTRIBUTORS SDN, BHD.
PHILIPPINES: National Book Store, Inc.
KOREA: Tongjin Chulpan Muyeok Co., Ltd.
INDONESIA: C.V. TOKO BUKU "MENTENG"
INDIA: Dani Book Land, Bombay 14
AUSTRALIA: BOOKWISE INTERNATIONAL
GUAM, SIPAN AND MICRONESIAN ISLANDS: FUJIWARA'S SALES & SERVICE
CANADA: MILESTONE PUBLICATIONS
U.S.A.: MASA T. & ASSOCIATES

ISBN4-915831-35-3

INTRODUCTION

Sandwiches can be the most complete and satisfying mini-meal in the world, simple to complex and elegant. They are quick and easy to prepare and are well-suited to today's life styles.

They are great favorites for lunches, picnics and as appetizers or main courses for all from the child with the peanut butter and jelly quick-fix to the most involved creations.

Everyone knows that a loaf of bread fresh from the oven always tastes the best, and modern equipment, techniques, and ingredients enable nearly anyone to produce a sandwich that is as good or better than any commercially produced. Excellent sandwich breads in loaf, Pita breads (pocket), or roll forms are all readily available at the supermarket or bakery today.

This book will guide you through simple techniques for preparing sandwiches for any occasion. The recipes in this collection are presented in step-by-step instruction form with pictures.

To serve luncheon sandwiches, present them artfully arranged on an appropriate, decorated serving platter. It is correctly stated that, "We eat first with the eyes". Many sandwich fillings can be prepared a day or two before use and refrigerated.

It is my pleasure to share these recipes so that you may have fun making a wholesome and attractive offering...

January, 1992

Yukiko Moriyama

CONTENTS

ACKNOWLEDGMENTS

I acknowledge with gratitude the contributions of the following people through their moral support, encouragement, and patience in the months required for the preparation of this publication.

To MR. SHIRO SHIMURA, publisher of JOIE, INC., and his wonderful staff for their trust and faith in my work.

A special debt of thanks is owned my collaborator, MIKE CHAPDELAINE, who helped me immensely in development of new recipes. The same thanks are also gratefully extended to MR. THOMAS CHAPDELAINE, and Mike's brother DAVID, who together own and operate the "CHAPPY'S" sandwich shop in Tampa, Florida, for sharing some of their recipes for this book.

To AKIRA NAITO and ATSUKO SAGARA, whose editorial assistance was indispensable……their hard work and dedication are much appreciated, and have been keys to the success of my projects.

To ATSUKO MURATA and KOH MINAGAWA, whose sense of design and illustration are much appreciated.

To MASAO TOKUYAMA, whose photographic talents are readily evident as being of the highest caliber.

A special place is always reserved for MRS. EIKO OHISHI, whose hard work and help in the kitchen is always so appreciated.

BASIC COOKING INFORMATION

1 cup is equivalent to 240 ml in our recipes: (American cup measurement)
1 American cup = 240 ml = 8 American fl oz
1 British cup = 200 ml = 7 British fl oz
1 Japanese cup = 200 ml
1 tablespoon = 15 ml   1 teaspoon = 5 ml

ABBREVIATIONS USED IN THIS BOOK

C = cup (s)	T = tablespoon (s)	t = teaspoon (s)	fl = fluid	oz = ounce (s)
lb (s) = pound (s)	ml = milliliter	g = grams	in = inch (es)	cm = centimeter
F = Fahrenheit	C = Celsius	doz = dozen	pkg (s) = package (s)	
pt (s) = pint (s)	qt (s) = quart (s)			

TABLES CONVERTING FROM U.S. CUSTOMARY SYSTEM TO METRICS

Liquid Measures

U.S. Customary system	oz	g	ml
1/16 cup = 1 T	1/2 oz	14 g	15 ml
1/4 cup = 4 T	2 oz	60 g	59 ml
1/2 cup = 8 T	4 oz	115 g	118 ml
1 cup = 16 T	8 oz	225 g	236 ml
1 3/4 cups	14 oz	400 g	414 ml
2 cups = 1 pint	16 oz	450 g	473 ml
3 cups	24 oz	685 g	710 ml
4 cups	32 oz	900 g	946 ml

Liquid Measures

Japanese system	oz	ml
1/8 cup	7/8 oz	25 ml
1/4 cup	1 3/4 oz	50 ml
1/2 cup	3 1/2 oz	100 ml
1 cup	7 oz	200 ml
1 1/2 cups	10 1/2 oz	300 ml
2 cups	14 oz	400 ml
3 cups	21 oz	600 ml
4 cups	28 oz	800 ml

Weights

ounces to grams*
1/4 oz = 7 g
1/2 oz = 14 g
1 oz = 30 g
2 oz = 60 g
4 oz = 115 g
6 oz = 170 g
8 oz = 225 g
16 oz = 450 g

*Equivalent

Linear Measures

inches to centimeters
1/2 in = 1.27 cm
1 in = 2.54 cm
2 in = 5.08 cm
4 in = 10.16 cm
5 in = 12.7 cm
10 in = 25.4 cm
15 in = 38.1 cm
20 in = 50.8 cm

Temperatures

Fahrenheit (F) to Celsius (C)		
freezer storage	−10°F =	−23.3°C
	0°F =	−17.7°C
water freezes	32°F =	0 °C
	68°F =	20 °C
	100°F =	37.7°C
water boils	212°F =	100 °C
	300°F =	148.8°C
	400°F =	204.4°C

Deep-Frying Oil Temperatures

300°F − 330°F (150°C − 165°C) = low	
340°F − 350°F (170°C − 175°C) = moderate	
350°F − 360°F (175°C − 180°C) = high	

Oven Temperatures

250°F − 350°F (120°C − 175°C) = low or cool	
350°F − 400°F (175°C − 204°C) = moderate or medium	
400°F − 450°F (204°C − 230°C) = hot	
450°F − 500°F (230°C − 260°C) = very hot	

SANDWICH BOOK

INGREDIENTS

BREADS

1. Long Italian loaf (Baquette)
2. French bread
3. Hoagy rolls (Poor boy French bread)
4. Rye bread
5. Whole-grain bread
6. English muffin
7. Hot dog bun
8. Wholewheat bun
9. Dinner rolls
10. Kaiser roll
11. Wholewheat bread
12. White sandwich bread
13. Dark sandwich bread
14. Pumpernickel bread
15. Rye bread
16. 7-grain bread
17. Rye crisp
18. White bread (unsliced)
19. Tortilla
20. Pita (pocket bread)
21. Taco shell
22. Whole pumpernickel bread
23. Whole-grain bread
24. Whole sourdough bread
25. Bagel
26. Rye bread (unsliced)
27. Hamburger bun
28. Brioch
29. Crescent roll
30. Oat bran bread
31. Granola bread
32. Raisin bread
33. White thick-slice bread
34. Oatmeal bread
35. Corn bread

See page 90, 92 for information

CHEESE

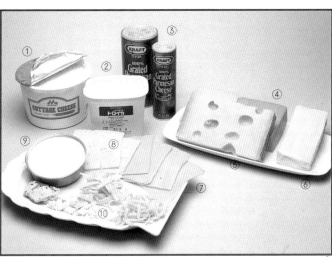

1. Cottage cheese
2. Sour cream
3. Parmesan cheese
4. Cheddar cheese
5. Swiss cheese (Emmenthaler)
6. White cheddar cheese
7. American process cheddar cheese
8. Monterey cheese
9. Cream cheese
10. Mozzarella cheese

BREAKFAST SANDWICH

This is a good breakfast recipe.

INGREDIENTS: Serves 1

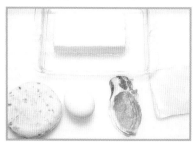

1   English muffin
1T butter or margarine
1   slice Canadian bacon or
1   sausage patty
1   egg
1   slice American cheese

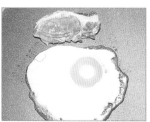

1. Split muffin in half; spread butter.

2. Heat teflon-coated griddle to medium. Break egg on a griddle; cook egg until egg white sets.

3. Fry Canadian bacon on both sides.

4. Toast muffins.

5. Turn egg over to finish frying.

6. Place cheese on top of egg.

7. Place bacon/cheese/egg on one toasted & buttered muffin slice.

8. Cover with other half of muffin & serve.

This is one of the most popular sandwich.

INGREDIENTS: Serves 1

3 oz (90g) corned beef
1¼ oz (45g) sauerkraut
2   slices Swiss cheese
2   slices rye bread
2T Thousand Island Dressing
1t mustard (optional)
1T butter or margarine

VARIATION: *Use Russian Dressing instead of Thousand Island Dressing.*

1. Put corned beef into microwave bowl.

2. Place sauerkraut on top.

3. Then top off with Swiss cheese slices.

4. Toast bread as preferred. Spread Thousand Island Dressing. Set aside.

5. Heat filling in microwave oven, uncovered, until cheese melts (approx. 45 sec. on high).

6. Remove corned beef from oven. Place 1 slice of rye bread over bowl, flip onto sandwich board.

7. Cover meat with other slice of bread.

8. For grilled flavor, coat both sides of toasted bread with butter and grill in preheated pan (medium heat) for one minute or until lightly browned on both sides.

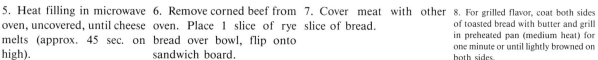

MEATY GRILLED CHEESE

Crispy bacon and melted cheese make a fine combination.

INGREDIENTS: Serves 1

- 2 slices bread, wheat or rye
- 2 slices American cheese
- 1 slice ham
- 1 slice bacon
- 2 slices tomato
- 1T butter or margarine

VARIATION: *Add mustard if you prefer.*

1

1. Lightly toast bread. Butter both pieces of toast and coat the opposite sides with mayonnaise.

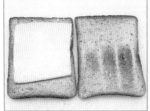

2

2. On mayonnaise coated side of toast, place cheese.

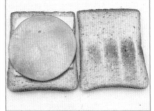

3

3. Place tomato slices and ham on top.

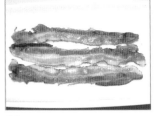

4

4. Fry bacon on medium heat or cook in microwave oven. Set on paper towel to soak up grease. Set aside.

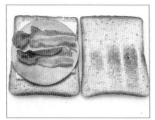

5

5. Place cooked bacon.

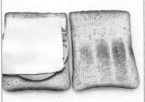

6

6. Place another slice of cheese on top.

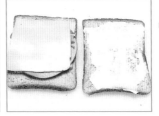

7

7. Cover with other piece of toast with butter on outside.

8

8. Grill on medium heat until cheese melts.

SCRAMBLED EGG MUFFIN SANDWICH

Good for luncheon or brunch with garden fresh vegetable salad.

INGREDIENTS: Serves 1

1 English muffin
2 slices bacon
2 fresh mushrooms
1 oz (30g) shredded Mozzarella cheese
1 egg
1T milk
Salt & pepper to taste
1-2 drops Tabasco sauce
1T butter or margarine
2t mayonnaise

1. Split muffin in half; toast lightly and spread with butter.

2. Fry bacon over medium heat or cook in microwwave oven. Set on papertowel to soak up grease. Set aside.

3. Slice mushrooms.

4. Break egg into a bowl; add mushrooms and 1T milk. Season with salt and pepper. Beat lightly. Add Tabasco sauce.

5. Melt butter in skillet over medium heat.

6. Pour in egg mixture all at once. Stir and mix until egg is set but still moist on the surface.

7. Spoon scrambled egg onto the bottom half of the muffin. Place cooked bacon on top.

8. Cover with other half of muffin.

SPICY GRILLED HAM & BACON

Kimchee is Korea's most traditional condiment.

INGREDIENTS: Serves 1

1	Kaiser roll or hamburger bun
3	strips of bacon
2	oz (60g) ham, 2 slices
1	oz (30g) Kimchee*
1T	Kimchee juice base
1/8	portion red pepper
2	slices Swiss cheese
1T	mayonnaise

Hot spicy cabbage is available at most Oriental grocery stores.

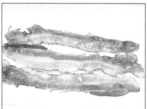

1

1. Cook bacon in microwave oven for 1½ minutes or fry bacon strips in pre-heated skillet; pour off grease. Set aside.

2

2. Cut red pepper into thin strips. Set aside.

3

3. Heat skillet over medium heat; place ham and pour in Kimchee juice base.

4

4. Add red pepper.

5

5. Add Kimchee and stir-fry for 1 to 2 minutes. Pour off excess juice.

6

6. Cut Kaiser roll in half. Spread on mayonnaise.

7

7. Place Swiss cheese, 1 slice of ham, and half portion of Kimchee mixture onto bottom slice of roll.

8

8. Place bacon strips on top.

9. Cover with other slice of ham and Kimchee mixture.

10. Top with other slice of cheese. Microwave 1 minute on high or until cheese melts. Serve hot.

HOT PASTRAMI ON DARK RYE BREAD

One of the best known and most popular sandwiches.

INGREDIENTS: Serves 1

2   slices dark rye bread
2   slices pastrami
2T sauerkraut
1   slice Swiss cheese
1T butter or margarine

1. Butter bread on outer surfaces. Place pastrami slices on unbuttered side of bread.

2. Place sauerkraut.

3. Place Swiss cheese on top.

4. Cover with other slice of bread. Place in pre-heated skillet (med) until lightly toasted, turn over & repeat on other side.

CHAPPY'S CHOICE

This enchanting combination of roast beef and cheese can be served as a hearty lunch.

INGREDIENTS: Serves 1

1   Kaiser roll or onion roll
4 oz (115g) roast beef, thinly sliced
1 oz (30g) mushroom
1 oz (30g) sweet onion or red onion
2   slices Swiss cheese
1T Au Jus
1T butter or margarine to saute mushrooms
$1/2$t horseradish
2T mayonnaise
    Dash of pepper

VARIATION: *Use sliced chicken or turkey in place of roast beef.*

1. Cut mushrooms into thin slices. Melt butter in skillet; saute mushrooms as desired. Set aside.

2. Slice onion into thin rounds.

3. Place roast beef into microwave howl. Add pepper. Add mushrooms and onion on top of beef. Then place cheese on top.

4. Place bowl in microwave oven and heat uncovered, on high for 45 seconds until cheese has melted.

5. Cut Kaiser roll in half (toast if preferred). Mix mayonnaise and horseradish together.

6. Coat both slices of roll with mayonnaise/horseradish sauce.

7. Place top half of roll over bowl and then flip-over contents onto sandwich board.

8. Place other half of roll over roast beef. Turn over sandwich: slice in half if desired.

16

SPICY BBQ BEEF ON A BUN

Marinade sauce can be used for chicken and spare ribs.

1. Slice bun in half. Set aside.

2. Marinate thinly sliced beef in marinade sauce for 5 minutes.

INGREDIENTS: 1 serving

1 hamburger bun
$1/4$lb (100g) thinly sliced beef, sirloin tip
1T oil
Marinade sauce:
1 clove garlic, minced
1t fresh ginger root, grated
1T soy sauce
$1/2$T brown sugar
1 drop Tabasco sauce
1T vegetable oil

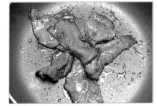

3. Heat 1T oil in skillet at medium heat: cook the meat, along with the marinade, until done.

4. Warm hamburger bun, top with meat and juice & enjoy.

FRENCH DIP SANDWICH

This sandwich can be served at an intimate brunch party for two.

1. Slice roll in half length wise.
Spread horseradish on both sides.

2. Fill Hoagy roll with roast beef; wrap sandwich in plastic wrap and microwave on high for 45 seconds or bake in aluminum foil at 350F (175C) for 10 minutes.

INGREDIENTS: 1-2 servings

1 Hoagy roll
4-6 oz (115-170g) roast beef
1T horseradish
1 cup Au Jus
or 1 beef bouillion cube with
$3/4$ cup water or $1/2$can beef broth
1T red wine

3. Unwrap and cut into half. Heat Au Jus to 190F (80 C).

4. Dip sandwich in Au Jus and enjoy.

SWEETHEART CHEESEBURGER

Everyone's all time favorite.

INGREDIENTS: Makes 2 burgers

4 slices bread
1/2 lb (225 g) lean ground beef
1 small egg, beaten
1t minced onion
1/2t salt
Dash of pepper
2 slices American cheese

1

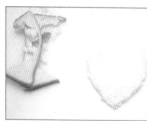

2

3

4

1. With large heart shaped cookie cutter, cut the centers from 4 slices of bread; toast lightly.

2. Make bread crumbs from the remaining pieces.

3. Add bread crumbs into ground beef.

4. Mix beaten egg with minced onion, salt and pepper.

5

6

7

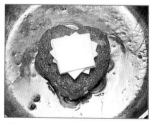

8

5. Combine egg mixture with ground beef and bread crumbs.

Divide mixture into 2 portions; stuff each portion into cookie cutter to shape.

7. Fry or grill meat on both sides.

8. Place cheese on top of the meat and serve on lightly toasted hearts.

CHEESEBURGERS

This cheeseburger is nearly everyone's favorite and truly an international fare.

INGREDIENTS: Makes 2 burgers

2 hamburger buns
1/2 lb (225 g) leaan ground beef
1 egg, lightly beaten
1/3 cup bread crumbs
Salt and pepper to taste
2 slices American cheddar cheese

1T butter or margarine
1T mayonnaise or mustard
1/2 T vegetable oil for grilling

GARNISHES:
Olives
Pickles
Lettuce
Tomato slices
Onion slices

1. Mix ground beef with egg, bread crumbs and salt & pepper.

2. Divide mixture into four portions; make 4 patties.

3. Fry or grill the meat on both sides. Place cheese on top of meat.

4. Slice buns; grill or toast. Coat with butter and mayonnaise or mustard.

19

SURPRISE CHEESEBURGER

Popular cheeseburger turned into a modern version.

INGREDIENTS: Makes 2 burgers

2 Kaiser rolls or hamburger buns

Ⓐ
- ½ lb (225g) lean ground beef
- ½ cup bread crumbs
- 1T steak sauce
- ½ cup tomato juice
- 2T shredded Mozzarella cheese
- Salt and pepper to taste

2 slices onion, chopped (about 1T)
1T butter or margarine
2T tomato ketchup

GARNISHES:
Black or green olives
Pickles

1

1. Divide ground meat in half, then divide again into four patties.

2

2. Chop onion.

3

3. Mix all Ⓐ ingredients and onion together.

4

4. Place half of mixture on one patty.

5

5. Place another patty on top and pinch edges to seal.

6

6. Repeat for second burger.

7

7. Grill burgers for 5 to 6 minutes on each side or until done.

8

8. Slice Kaiser rolls; grill or toast. Coat with butter. Place grilled burgers on bottom of rolls. Top with ketchup and olives or pickles if desired.

This cheese combination makes an ideal brunch dish.

INGREDIENTS: Makes 1 bagel

1   bagel
1   slice Swiss cheese
1   slice Cheddar cheese
1   slice Provalone cheese
2t peppercorn dressing or creamy
    salad dressing
1t Parmesan cheese
1T butter or margarine

1

1. Mix salad dressing with Parmesan cheese. Set aside.

2

2. Cut bagel in half and toast lightly; brush with butter.

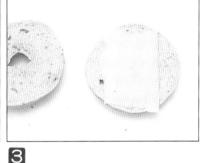

3

3. Place Swiss cheese on bottom half of bagel.

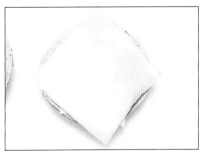

4

4. Place cheddar cheese on top.

5

5. Place Provalone cheese.

6

6. Spread dressing mixture on top.

21

BEANS & FRANKS

One of the easiest hot dog dishes to prepare for a fine light meal.

INGREDIENTS: Makes 2 hot dogs

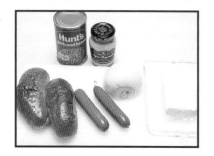

2	hot dog buns	1¼ cups pork and beans
2t	butter or margarine	1T chopped onion
2	wieners	½ t prepared mustard

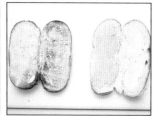

1. Grill or boil wieners.

2. Heat pork and beans.

3. Toast or heat hot dog buns. Coat with butter and mustard.

4. Place wiener into each bun. Spoon heated pork and beans on top and sprinkle with chopped onion. Serve hot.

SAUERKRAUT & FRANKS

This is German version of a hot dog.

INGREDIENTS: Makes 1 hot dog

1 hot dog bun
1T butter or margarine
1 wiener
1T ketchup
1 dill pickle
1t mustard
2T sauerkraut

1. Make a few diagonal slashes in weiner and grill or boil as shown.

2. Cut bun halfway through, lengthwise, as shown.

3. Toast bun; coat with butter. Place sauerkraut and wiener in bun. Serve with ketchup, pickle and mustard.

SALAMI & SAUERKRAUT

It can be prepared in minutes.

INGREDIENTS: Serves 1

1 hot dog bun
1T butter or margarine
2 slices salami
1 slice Swiss cheese, cut in half
2T sauerkraut

VARIATION: *Broil until cheese melts.*

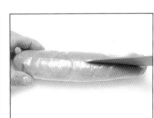

1. Cut center top of hot dog bun halfway through, lengthwise, as shown.

2. Heat bun; coat with butter or margarine. Fill with salami and cheese slices.

3. Place sauerkraut on top. Place in 350°F (175°C) oven for 3 minutes or until cheese melts.

23

CRESCENT ROLL HOT DOG

This makes a filling, tasty lunch with milk or juice.

INGREDIENTS: Makes 4 rolls

4 sheets of crescent roll dough
4 wieners
4 slices American cheese

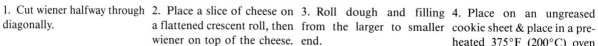

1. Cut wiener halfway through diagonally.

2. Place a slice of cheese on a flattened crescent roll, then wiener on top of the cheese.

3. Roll dough and filling from the larger to smaller end.

4. Place on an ungreased cookie sheet & place in a preheated 375°F (200°C) oven for 12 minutes.

CRABMEAT & CHEESE ROLL

This lovely combination of cheese and crabmeat can be served as an appetizer.

INGREDIENTS: Makes 4 rolls

1 pie sheet, 8-in (20 cm) square
4 sticks immitation crabmeat (sea leg)
2 slices Swiss cheese

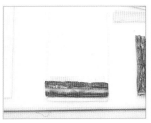

1. Cut pie sheet into fourths, 2-in (5 cm) wide as shown above.

2. Cut cheese into halves. Place a slice of cheese on a pie sheet, then 1 stick crabmeat on top of cheese.

3. Roll up.

4. Place on an ungreased cookie sheet and bake in preheated 375°F (200°C) oven for 12 minutes.

FRENCH TOAST

This simple yet hearty toast can be served any time.

INGREDIENTS: Makes 2 Slices

2 slices bread
2 eggs
1/2 cup milk
1T sugar

A dash of cinnamon powder
A pinch of salt
2T butter or margarine

VARIATION: *Add cooked bacon bits to egg mixture.*

1. Break eggs into a small bowl; add milk and beat lightly.

2. Add sugar, cinnamon powder and salt.

3. Dip bread into egg mixture.

4. Melt butter in skillet over medium heat and slide bread into skillet. Cook 2 minutes on each side or until egg mixture is set.

MAYONNAISE TOAST

Low calorie mayonnaise can also be used.

INGREDIENTS: Makes 2 rolls

2   Kaiser or onion rolls
1T mayonnaise
1T Parmesan cheese

1

1. Mix mayonnaise with Parmesan cheese.

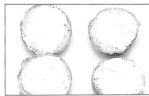

2

2. Split rolls into halves. Spread mayonnaise mixture on top. Broil until lightly browned.

HOT SALAMI WITH PARMESAN CHEESE

Mayonnaise with Parmesan cheese adds texture and flavor.

INGREDIENTS: Makes 2 rolls

2 dinner rolls
2 slices salami
Ⓐ { 1T mayonnaise
    1t Parmesan cheese
    1t minced parsley

1

1. Cut rolls into halves. Mix Ⓐ ingredients together; coat both bottom and top portion of roll with mixture.

2

2. Add salami, broil top and bottom separately. Combine & serve.

27

VEGETABLE CROQUETTE SANDWICH

These croquettes can be served as a main dish.

INGREDIENTS: makes 2 sandwiches

2   dinner rolls or hamburger buns
2T butter or margarine
²/₃ cup mashed potato mix

Ⓐ { 1T butter or margarine
    ¹/₄t salt
    ¹/₃ cup milk
    ²/₃ cup water

¹/₂ Japanese cucumber, thinly sliced or ¹/₄ cup chopped cucumber
¹/₄ cup carrot, shredded
A   dash of pepper
¹/₄ cup all-purpose flour
1   egg, lightly beaten
¹/₄ cup bread crumbs
Vegetable oil for deep-frying
2   lettuce leaves (optional)

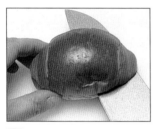

1

1. Split rolls in half; toast rolls and butter.

2

2. Heat Ⓐ ingredients; stir in mashed potato mix until moistened. Add cucumber and carrot.

3

3. Divide into two patties.

4. Coat patties with flour.

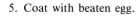

5

5. Coat with beaten egg.

6

6. Coat with bread crumbs.

7

7. Deep-fry in oil at 340°– 360°F (170°–180°C) until golden brown. Drain on wire rack.

8

8. Place butter cup-lettuce on roll and place croquette on top.

This recipe adds a festive touch to an intimate party.

INGREDIENTS: 2 Servings

1 loaf sourdough bread
2-3 T butter or margarine
1 clove garlic, crushed
1t minced parsley
2 cooked potato croquettes (see page 28)

VARIATION: *Meatballs can be used.*

1

1. Cut top quarter from bread and set aside.

2

2. Remove all but ½ in layer of bread from inside crust. Leftover portion can be used to make bread crumbs.

3

3. Soften butter at room temperature; add crushed garlic.

4

4. Add minced parsley.

5

5. Coat the inside and top quater of bread with butter mixture.

6

6. Bake for 5 minutes in preheated 350°F (175°C) oven. Place cooked croquettes in bread basket.

7

7. Slice and serve.

MEXICAN CHICKEN ENCHILADAS

This much-admired enchilada dish makes an ideal brunch or dinner entre.

INGREDIENTS: Makes 4 enchiladas

4   flour tortilla
10   oz (300g) chicken breast, de-boned, skinless
1t   oil

(A)
- $^1/_2$ cup shredded Monterey Jack cheese
- $^1/_4$ cup sour cream
- 1 green onion, chopped
- 1T minced parsley

(B)
- 1 can (8oz, 225g) tomato sauce
- $^1/_4$ cup chopped green pepper
- 1T chopped green chili
- $^1/_2$ small ripe tomato, chopped
- 1t chili powder
- $^1/_8$t ground cumin

$^1/_2$ cup Monterey Jack cheese, shredded
1T   chopped pitted green or black olives

1

1. Cut chicken breast into thin slices.

2

2. Heat 1t oil in skillet over medium heat; cook & stir fry until done.

3

3. Mix (A) ingredients.

4

4. Add mixed (A) ingredients with chicken; divide into fourths.

5

5. Prepare tortillas according to the package direction. Place chicken mixture on each tortilla.

6

6. Roll the tortilla.

7

7. Place in a baking dish seam side down.

8

8. Mix all (B) ingredients; cook over medium heat for 5 minutes.

9

9. Pour sauce over enchiladas.

10

10. Sprinkle with ¹/₂ cup cheese. Bake, uncovered, in 350°F (175°C) oven about 15 minutes or until bubbly. Garnish with chopped olives.

NOTE: *place 4 enchiladas in ungreased oblong baking dish, 12″ × 7″ × 2″ (30.5 × 9 × 5 cm)*

GRILLED BEEF & CHEDDAR

Roast beef is often served as a main dish.

INGREDIENTS: Serves 1 to 2

1 French or Hoagy roll
4 oz (115 g) roast beef
¹/₂ oz (15 g) red onion
¹/₂ green pepper, thinly sliced
1 slice cheddar cheese
1T Teriyaki sauce
Dash of pepper
1T mayonnaise

1

1. Marinate roast beef in Teriyaki sauce for 5 minutes.

2

2. Cut onion into thin rounds.

3

3. Grill roast beef with green pepper and onion.

4

4. Place cheese slice over ingredients to allow for melting before turning off heat, about 30 seconds. Cut French bread in half lengthwise; coat with mayonnaise. Place grilled ingredients on bread.

31

TUNA MELT

This tuna melt fits perfectly in a party menu.

INGREDIENTS: Serves 4 to 6

- 1 loaf Italian bread
- 1 6½ oz (185 g) can tuna, drained, flaked
- ¼ cup celery, chopped
- 1 green onion, sliced diagonally
- 2 pimiento stuffed olives, chopped
- ½T sunflower seeds
- ¼ cup mushrooms
- ¼ cup low-fat mayonnaise or salad dressing of your choice
- 2 cheddar cheese slices, cut in half lengthwise

1. Cut mushrooms into thin slices.

2. Mix flaked tuna with celery, green onion, olives, sunflower seeds and sliced mushrooms.

3. Add mayonnaise and mix well.

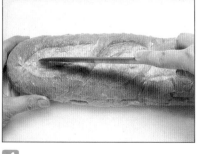

4. Cut center of bread lengthwise, being careful not to cut through bottom crust.

5. Place cheese slices in shell.

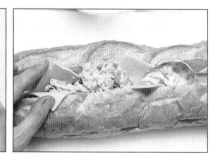

6. Fill with tuna mixture.
Wrap in foil. Pre-heat oven to 375°F (200°C). Bake for 10 minutes or until cheese melts.

PORK CUTLET SANDWICH

This cutlet is crispy outside and moist inside.

INGREDIENTS: Makes 1 sandwich

2 slices bread
1/2 lb (225 g) boneless pork tenderloin
A pinch of salt & dash of pepper
All-purpose flour for dusting
1 egg, lightly beaten with 1/2 t water
1/4 cup bread crumbs
Vegetable oil for deep-frying
2T Worcestershire sauce
1/2T Ketchup

1

1. Remove excess fat; make slits along pork to prevent shrinkage while cooking.

2

2. Sprinkle with salt and pepper.

3

3. Dust pork fillet with all-purpose flour.

4

4. Dip into beaten egg.

5

5. Then coat with bread crumbs. Press on both sides.

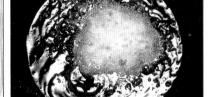

6

6. Heat deep-frying oil to 340°F (170°C). Deep-fry pork until done or golden brown. Drain excess grease on paper towel. Mix worcestershire sauce and ketchup and serve with cutlet.

CHICKEN CUTLET SANDWICH

This chicken cutlet is very tasty and easy to make.

INGREDIENTS: Makes 2 sandwiches

Repeat same process as pork cutlet.
Use 1/2 lb (225 g) chicken breast (deboned and skinless) in place of pork fillet.

CLUB SANDWICH

This colorful sandwich is ideal for lunch.

INGREDIENTS: 2 servings

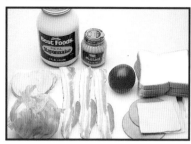

3 slices of favorite bread
2 oz (60 g) sliced roast chicken
    breast
2 slices ham
3 slices bacon
2 slices tomato
2 lettuce leaves
1T mayonnaise
1T mustard
1T butter or margarine (optional)
2 slices of favorite cheese

1

2

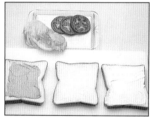

3

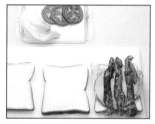

4

1. In skillet, fry bacon strips.

2. Or cook in microwave oven on high for 2 minutes. Set aside.

3. Slice tomato to preferred thickness; wash and pat dry lettuce. Spread butter, mustard and mayonnaise on separate slices of bread.

4. Place lettuce, ham, and bacon on top of bread (either slice coated with mayonnaise or mustard).

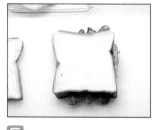

5

6

7

8

5. Cover with one slice of bread.

6. Place chicken and cheese on top of bread.

7. Add tomato and lettuce.

8. Cover with other slice of bread. Cut into quarters at 90° angle. Put toothpicks into center of each quarter. Serve with chips and pickle.

Leftover roast turkey makes an excellent sandwich.

INGREDIENTS: Serves 1 to 2

2   slices rye bread or pumpernick-
    el bread
3oz (90g) turkey breast
1oz (30g) ham
2   slices Swiss cheese
1   cup uncooked spinach leaves
1T butter or margarine
Sandwich spread:
3t Dijon mustard
1½t mayonnaise
1t Parmesan cheese

1

1. In skillet, melt butter over medium heat; add spinach and sauté for 1 minute. Set aside.

2

2. Place both ham and turkey into microwave-safe dish.

3

3. Place spinach, then cheese on top. Cook in microwave oven for 10 to 15 seconds or until cheese melts.

4

4. Mix Dijon mustard with mayonnaise in a small cup. Add 1t Parmesan cheese.

5

5. Coat both slices of bread with Dijon sauce.

6

6. Cover the dish with bread slice; turn over, flip method.

7

Cover with other slice of bread. Cut into halves and serve.

TURKEY CLUB SANDWICH

This is a very simple and popular sandwich.

INGREDIENTS: 1 to servings

3   thin bread slices
1 or 2 strips bacon
1   slice turkey
1   slice cheese
2   slices tomato
1   lettuce leaf
$1/2$ cup alfalfa sprouts
2T mayonnaise
1T Dijon mustard
1T butter or margarine

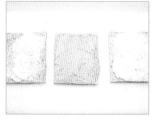

1

1. Spread butter, mustard and mayonnaise on separate slices of bread.

2

2. Place leaf of lettuce and crispy cooked bacon on a slice of bread.

3

3. Add tomato slices.

4

4. Cover with second piece of bread, mustard side down.

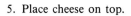

5

5. Place cheese on top.

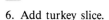

6

6. Add turkey slice.

7

7. Sprinkle alfalfa sprouts on top.

8

8. Cover with the third piece of bread; cut into halves and serve.

TURKEY & SWISS

Popular ingredients make one of the all-time international favorite sandwiches.

INGREDIENTS: 1 to 2 servings

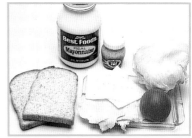

2   slices wheat bread
4oz (115g) turkey
2   slices Swiss cheese
1T mayonnaise
1T mustard
Lettuce & tomato (optional)

1. Coat both slices of bread with mayonnaise and mustard.

2. Place turkey on one bread slice.

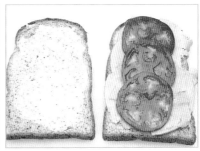

3. Add tomato slices.

4. Top off with Swiss cheese.

5. Add lettuce leaf, if you prefer.

6. Cover with other piece of bread; cut diagonally and serve.

BASIC EGG SALAD SANDWICH

This sandwich can be served as a delightful vegetarian dish.

INGREDIENTS: Makes 1 egg salad sandwich

2 slices white or wheat bread
2 eggs
$1/8$ cup chopped celery
2T mayonnaise
Dash of paprika
1T butter or margarine

VARIATION: *Add lettuce and tomato slices. Serve with pumpernickel bread.*

1. Hardboil 2 eggs.

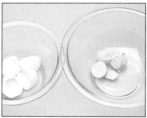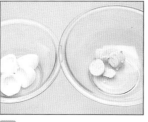

2. Cut in half after removing shells; separate yolk and white.

3. Crumble egg yolk.

4. Chop egg white and mix with yolk.

5. Add chopped celery and mix well.

6. Add mayonnaise and dash of paprika.

7. Spread onto bread slice lightly coated with butter.

8. Cover with other bread slice. Cut in half and serve.

FANCY EGG SALAD SANDWICH

It is simple to make, yet very nutritious and elegant.

INGREDIENTS: Makes 2 sandwiches

2   crescent rolls
1   cup basic egg salad recipe (page 38) with chopped celery omitted.
1t   chopped onion
1T   carrot, chopped
2T   chopped cucumber

1

2

3

1. Prepare egg salad as directed on page 32.

2. Mix in vegetables and mayonnaise with egg salad.

3. Cut crescent rolls into halves as shown. Spoon onto bottom portion of roll.

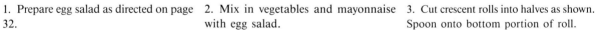

VARIATION: *Serve with your favorite bread.*

TERRINE & AVOCADO

This Terrine can be considered a gourmet sandwich.

INGREDIENTS: 1 to 2 servings

2 slices bread
2 slices terrine of your choice
1 slice Edam cheese
$\frac{1}{2}$ cup alfalfa sprouts
1 avocado
2T mayonnaise
1 lettuce leaf

1. Cut avocado lengthwise around the seed.

2. Twist gently to separate halves

3. Spoon out avocado from shell.

4. Sprinkle with lemon juice to prevent browning; chop up avocado and mix with mayonnaise.

5. Spread onto both slices of bread.

6. Place lettuce over avocado mix.

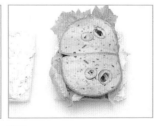

7. Add terrine slices.

8. Place Edam cheese on top.

9. Sprinkle alfalfa sprouts onto cheese.

10. Cover with other slice of bread. Cut at 90° angle.

B·L·T

BLT stands for bacon, lettuce and tomato. It sometimes can also be referred to as breakfast, lunch and teatime.

INGREDIENTS: 1 serving

2 slices bread
3 strips bacon
1 lettuce leaf
3 slices tomato
2t mayonnaise

VARIATION: *Add slice of favorite cheese. Use shredded lettuce instead of leaf lettuce.*

1. Toast bread slices lightly. Coat one slice with mayonnaise.

2. Cook bacon (see page 34). Place lettuce and tomato slices onto toast.

3. Place cooked bacon on top of tomato.

4. Cover with other piece of bread. Cut in half and serve with potato salad.

THE CUBAN

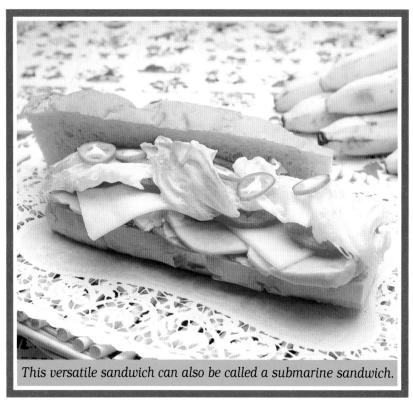

This versatile sandwich can also be called a submarine sandwich.

INGREDIENTS: 3 to 4 servings

1	loaf French bread
2	slices turkey
2	slices roasted pork
2	slices salami
2	slices Swiss cheese
1T	mayonnaise
1T	mustard
2	slices tomato
1	leaf lettuce
4	small pickle slices

VARIATION: *Wrap in foil and bake at 400°F (220°C) for 8 to 10 minutes, Or use microwave oven. Add lettuce and tomato after heating. You can add jalopena pepper for spiciness.*

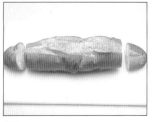

1

1. Cut 2″ (5 cm) off from both ends of the bread.

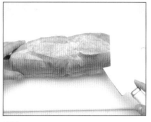

2

2. Cut in half lengthwise as shown.

3

3. Coat one side with mustard and other side with mayonnaise.

4

4. Place turkey and salami onto the half coated with mayonnaise.

5

5. Add cheese slices.

6

6. Top off with tomato and lettuce.

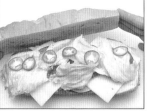

7

7. Cover with other piece of bread.

8

8. Cut into appropriate serving sizes.

ITALIAN EGG SALAD SANDWICH

This delightful recipe makes a colorful addition to your sandwich menu.

INGREDIENTS: Makes 1 hoagy loaf sandwich

1	loaf Italian or hoagy roll
1T	olive oil
2	hard boiled eggs
4	olives, pitted and chopped
1T	minced parsley
3	slices tomato

Ⓐ
- 2T mayonnaise
- 1t Dijon mustard
- ½ t salt
- 1t Parmesan cheese

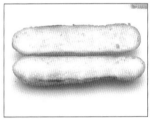

1

2

3

4

1. Cut bread into halves lengthwise as shown; toast lightly and brush with olive oil. Set aside.

2. Make basic egg salad page 38); mix with Ⓐ ingredients. Add chopped olives and minced parsley and mix together.

3. Place tomato slices onto the bottom portion of bread.

4. Place egg salad on top and cover with other piece of bread.

VARIATION: *Toasted English muffins can be used instead of a hoagy roll.*

43

BEEF TONGUE & TURKEY

COLD SANDWICH

The aroma of mild sesame Teriyaki sauce stimulates the appetite.

INGREDIENTS: Makes 1 sandwich

2   slices pumpernickel bread
2oz (60g) smoked beef tongue
2oz (60g) turkey slices
2T sesame Teriyaki sauce*
1T Thousand Island Dressing
* *Available at oriental grocery stores.*

VARIATION: *Add slice of Swiss cheese.*

1. Marinate beef tongue in Teriyaki sauce for 2 minutes.

2. Sauté beef tongue with sauce for 2–3 minutes.

3. Coat bread with Thousand Island Dressing.

4. Place turkey slices onto one slice of bread.

5. Place sautéd beef tongue on top. Cover with other slice. Cut into halves and serve.

44

SMOKED SALMON WITH BAGELS

Smoked salmon is outstanding with a crispy bagel.

INGREDIENTS: Makes 2 bagels

2   bagels
3   to 4 slices smoked salmon fillet
    or 1oz (30g) smoked salmon
2T cream cheese
2   slices red onion
1T capers

1. Cut bagel into halves; toast and coat with cream cheese.

2. Place smoked salmon slices onto one half.

3. Cut onion into thin rounds.

4. Place onion on top. Sprinkle some capers on top.

VARIATION: *Use Kaiser or onion roll instead of bagels.*

MANDARIN ORANGE & CHICKEN

The flavor of mandarin orange turns ordinary chicken into something special.

INGREDIENTS: Makes 1 sandwich

2   slices pumpernickel bread
3oz (90g) chicken breast, deboned, skinned
1t   low-salt soy sauce (optional)
4   slices mandarin orange
6   walnuts
1T   celery, chopped
1/8t dill spice
1T   mayonnaise

VARIATION: *Substitute mandarin orange with 1oz (30g) pineapple.*

1. Cook chicken in boiling water with 1t soy sauce until tender.

2. Mince chicken and place in mixing bowl. Chop walnuts and celery separately then place into bowl.

3. Mix-in dill spice and mayonnaise.

4. Place chopped mandarin orange slices into bowl with walnuts and celery then mix together.

5. Spread onto bread.

6. Cover with other slice of bread. Cut in half and serve.

LIVERWURST SANDWICH

Liverwurst can be served on crackers for appetizers or snacks.

1. Break up livewurst with fork in a bowl. Spread onto bottom portion of both crescent rolls.

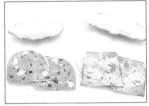

2. Place slices of terrine on top. Cover with top pieces of crescent rolls.

INGREDIENTS: Makes 2 sandwiches

- 2 crescent rolls
- 4¼ oz (120 g) German-style liverwurst spread
- 4 thin slices terrine

PEANUT BUTTER AND JELLY SANDWICH

An assortment of jam goes well with peanut butter.

1. Make 4 sandwiches, using peanut butter, strawberry jam, grape jam and marmalade as shown.

2. Stack sandwiches on top of each other and slice crosswise.

INGREDIENTS: 2 servings

- 8 thin slices sandwich bread, trimmed
- Peanut butter
- Strawberry jam
- Grape jam
- Orange marmalade

TUNA SALAD SANDWICH

COLD SANDWICH

There are many ways to prepare and serve tuna. This is one colorful and easy way to make a sandwich.

INGREDIENTS: Makes 1 sandwich

2   slices bread
2oz (60g) or 2T canned tuna, drained
1T chopped celery
1½T mayonnaise
Dash of pepper
2   small lettuce leaves
2   slices tomato

VARIATION: *Add favorite sliced cheese or add 1oz (30g) crushed pineapple*

1. Drain tuna; place tuna in a bowl.

2. Mix chopped celery with tuna.

3. Add mayonnaise; mix well.

4. Sprinkle with pepper.

5. Spread tuna mixture on a single slice of bread.

6. Add lettuce.

7. Place tomato slices over lettuce.

8. Place lettuce and top with other slice of bread. Cut in half and serve with potato chips and pickle.

LO-CAL TUNA SANDWICH

This low-calorie, high protein sandwich can be ideal for calorie conscious people.

INGREDIENTS: Serves 2

4-6 slices bread
2T butter or margarine
1 6½oz (185g) can of tuna (in water), drained and flaked
½ cup of cottage cheese
Light mayonnaise to taste

1 sweet pickle, diced
1t lemon juice
Dash of pepper
Sprinkle of paprika

1. Spread butter onto slices of bread. Chop sweet pickle into small pieces.

2. Mix flaked tuna with mayonnaise and diced sweet pickle.

3. Add lemon juice and sprinkle with dash of pepper and paprika; mix well.

4. Spoon onto single slice of buttered bread, cover with another slice; Cut in half and serve.

HAM & PINEAPPLE BAGEL

Americans have so long admired bagels for making wonderful sandwiches with different fillings.

INGREDIENTS: Serves 1

1   onion or plain bagel
1–2T   cream cheese
2–3   thinly sliced ham, turkey or
      chicken meat
1   pineapple ring

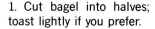

1. Cut bagel into halves; toast lightly if you prefer.

2. Spread cream cheese onto bagel.

3. Place sliced ham onto single bagel slice.

4. Top with pineapple ring. Cover with other bagel slice.

50

CREAM CHEESE DELIGHT

This sandwich can be made ahead of time for lunch.

INGREDIENTS: Serves 1 to 2

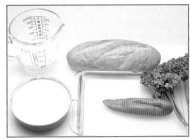

1 French loaf or Hoagy roll
^{2}/$_3$oz (20g) cod roe
4oz (115g) cream cheese
1t milk
1T minced parsley

VARIATION: *Wrap in plastic wrap and refrigerate to firm up or Slice and place in original shape and wrap.*

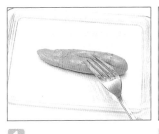

1

1. Pierce cod roe on both sides in several places with a fork to prevent shrinkage.

2

2. Cover with plastic wrap; microwave for 40–50 seconds on high. Unwrap and remove outer skin.

3

3. Cut bread into halves crosswise as shown. Pull out center of bread and save as bread crumbs for other recipes.

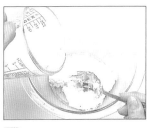

4

4. Mix cream cheese with 1t milk; stir well.

5

5. Add minced parsley.

6

6. Stuff cream cheese mixture into the bread. Cut slices with a sharp knife.

Serving suggestion: Spread onto crackers.

51

POTATO LOVERS SANDWICH

Potatoes are an all-time favorite for everyone.

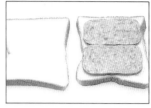

1. Spread butter onto both slices of bread.

2. Place lunch meat onto single slice of bread.

INGREDIENTS: Serves 1

2 slices of bread
1–2T butter or margarine
$^1/_2$–$^2/_3$ cup mashed potato (see page 53)
2 thick slices lunch meat of your choice or other meat slices

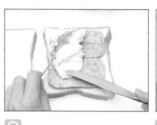

3. Spread mashed potato on top of meat.

4. Cover with other slice of buttered bread.

POTATO WITH BACON

Potato and bacon are an all-time favorite for everyone.

1. Split muffin into halves lengthwise.

2. Toast muffin; spread butter while still hot. Place mashed potato onto muffin.

INGREDIENTS: Serves 1

1 English muffin
1T butter or margarine
2 strips bacon, cooked
4T mashed potato (see page 53)

3. Place cooked bacon on top.

4. Cover with other piece of muffin.

ROLLED SANDWICH

Colorful fillings make this sandwich special.

INGREDIENTS: Serves 1

1 loaf unsliced bread
2T mashed potato (recipe below)
1/4 bunch of fresh spinach
1t Parmesan cheese
Salt & pepper to taste

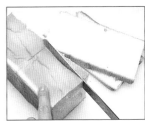

1. With a sharp knife, slice bread into 1-in (1.5 cm) thick slices lengthwise.

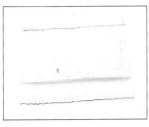

2. Trim off crust on both sides.

3. Cover bread with a layer of mashed potato.

4. Cook spinach and drain well. Cut into small pieces.

5. Place spinach onto mashed potato and sprinkle with Parmesan cheese, salt & pepper. Roll up. Wrap in plastic wrap and refrigerate for about 20 minutes. Cut into thin rounds with a sharp knife and serve.

▶ **MASHED POTATO**

INGREDIENTS: Serves 1

7 oz (200 g) baking potato, 1 medium-size potato
1/4 cup hot milk   1T butter
2/3t salt
Dash of pepper

1. Scrub potato well, pierce both sides in several places with a fork. Place potato in the center of microwave oven; cook on high for 4 to 5 minutes or fork tender.

2. Peel potato; place into a bowl and mash.

3. Add butter, hot milk and salt & pepper and beat into fluffy consistency.

INSTANT MASHED POTATOES
INGREDIENTS: Makes 1 cup

2/3 cup instant mashed potato mix
2/3 cup water
1T butter or margarine
1/4t salt
1/3 cut milk

1. In medium sauce pan, heat water, butter or margarine and salt to boiling. Remove from heat and add milk.

2. Stir in mashed potato mix.

3. Briskly stir with fork or wire whisk until soft and moist.

CRUNCHY VEGETABLE DELIGHT

COLD SANDWICH

The bright green and red provide a pleasant color contrast to this sandwich.

INGREDIENTS: Serves 2

2 English muffins or bagels
1 small Japanese cucumber or 3-in (7.5 cm) long English cucumber
$1/2$ tomato
$1/2$ cup alfalfa sprouts (substitute shredded lettuce)
Cream cheese
Dash of seasoned pepper

1. Slice cucumber and tomato into thin slices.

2. Cut muffins into halves.

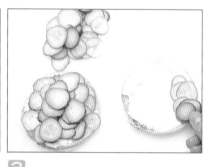

3. Lightly toast muffins or bagels; spread thickly with cream cheese.

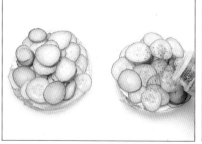

4. Arrange sliced cucumber on bottom sides of muffins or both halves of the bagels.

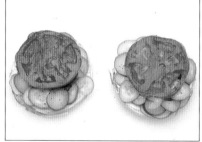

5. Add tomato slices.

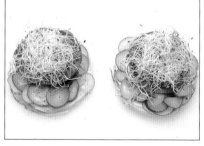

6. Add alfalfa sprouts on top. Cover with other muffin slices or bagel halves.

54

A touch of mustard adds zest to this sandwich.

INGREDIENTS: Makes 1 sandwich

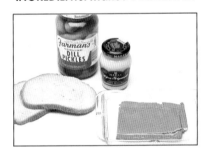

2   slices rye bread
1T spicy brown mustard or Dijon
    mustard
3½ to 4oz (100 to 115g) thinly
    sliced corned beef
3½oz (100g) dill pickle

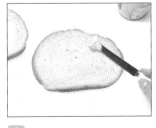
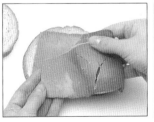

1. Spread mustard on one slice of bread.

2. Place corned beef onto bread.

3. Cut dill pickle into thin slices. Place on top of corned beef.

4. Place other slice of bread over pickles. Slice in half and serve.

SUBMARINE SANDWICH

Wrap in plastic wrap for lunch or picnic.

INGREDIENTS: Serves 4 to 6

1 Italian loaf of bread
2 to 3 T mayonnaise
2 to 3T mustard
3 to 4 slices salami
3 to 4 slices pastrami
4 slices turkey

4 slices ham
4 slices Swiss cheese
1½ cups shredded cabbage
1 tomato, sliced
1 pickle, sliced lengthwise

Garnishes: French-fry potatoes
Pickles
Potato chips

Condiments: Mayonnaise
Mustard
Ketchup

1

1. Cut bread into halves lengthwise. Coat one side with mayonnaise and the other with mustard.

2

2. Top with salami, pastrami, turkey, ham and Swiss cheese.

3

3. Add shredded cabbage, tomato and pickle slices. Cover with other half of loaf. Slice and serve.

56

CHILLED PORK SANDWICH

This makes a tasty, filling lunch with soup or salad.

INGREDIENTS: Serves 1

Available at Oriental grocery stores

2   slices rye sandwich bread
7 oz (200 g) thinly sliced pork loin
1T butter or margarine
1   leaf lettuce
3   slices cucumber
Dipping sauce:
Ⓐ
    1T peanut butter
    1T rice vinegar
    ¼t mirin or sake*
    1t sugar
    ¼t soy sauce

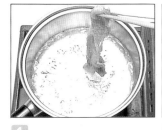  

1. Cook meat in boiling water for 3 to 4 minutes.

2. Dip into ice water. Set aside.

3. Mix Ⓐ ingredients.

4. Dip pork into the sauce. Toast bread lightly; spread butter on one side of the bread. Add lettuce leaf, cucumber slices and pork on top. Cover with other slice of bread. Cut in half and serve.

57

TORTILLA

Tortillas are thin round Mexican bread made of cornmeal or flour.

INGREDIENTS: Serves 2

2 tortilla or taco shells
1/4 lb (100 g) spicy BBQ beef, cooked (see page 17)
1/2 green pepper, chopped
1T sour cream
1T salsa or Taco sauce
1T chopped green onion & 1t minced parsley (optional)
1T Teriyaki sauce (see page 96)

VARIATION: *4 oz (100 g) thin sliced suk-iyaki beef*
1T Teriyaki sauce
1. Brown sukiyaki beef in skillet over medium heat; add Teriyaki sauce and cook 1 minute. Spoon beef-sauce mix on warmed tortilla.

1. Heat tortilla 4 or 5 minutes on both sides in oven (350°F, 175°C) or use skilleta as an option.

2. Pour *teriyaki* sauce into bowl and marinate beef for 5 minutes.

3. Place cooked beef on warmed tortilla.

4. Add chopped green pepper.

5. Add sour cream.

6. Top with salsa or taco sauce. Sprinkle with chopped green onion & mined parsley if you desire and serve.

ROLLED SMOKED SALMON

This dish can be served as an appetizer.

OPEN-FACE SANDWICH

INGREDIENTS: Serves 2

2   bagles
3   slices smoked salmon or 1 oz (30 g) smoked salmon fillet
1/4 Japanese cucumber*
4T cream cheese, softened

* *English cucumber can be used instead of Japanese kind. Cut into fourths lengthwise.*

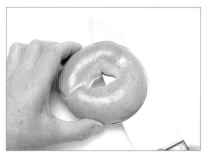

1. Cut bagels into halves.

2. Toast lightly; coat with softened cream cheese. Set aside.

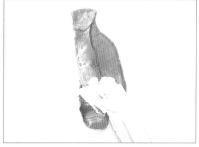

3. Spread cream cheese onto slices of smoked salmon.

4. Place cucumber on salmon as shown above.

5. Roll up.

6. Cut into 1-in (2.5 cm) thick slices; place on bagels and serve.

LUNCHMEAT & PINEAPPLE

A colorful appearance is something special.

INGREDIENTS: Serves 2

2 slices bread	1T cream cheese
2 leaves lettuce	2 slices pineapple ring
4 slices (1/2-in, 1.25 cm thick) Spam, corned beef or other lunchmeat	2 cherries

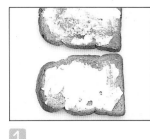  

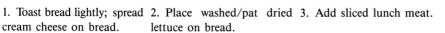

1. Toast bread lightly; spread cream cheese on bread.

2. Place washed/pat dried lettuce on bread.

3. Add sliced lunch meat.

4. Top both slices with one pineapple ring and cherry.

CALIFORNIAN OPEN-FACE SANDWICH

A popular lunch dish in California.

INGREDIENTS: Serves 1

1	slice bread	2	slices avocado
3oz (90g) turkey slices		1	slice Monterey Jack cheese
2	slices tomato	1	slice cheddar cheese ½oz (15g)
			Almond slices

1. Place turkey on single slice of bread.

2. Add tomato slices onto turkey slices.

3. Add Monterey Jack cheese slice.

4. Stack avocado slices and cheddar cheese slice on top. Heat in toaster oven/microwave on high until cheese melts, about 45 seconds to 1 minute. Sprinkle with almond slices.

61

CHICKEN ON WHEAT BREAD

Yogurt with dill weed provide flavor.

INGREDIENTS: Serves 1

1   slice wheat bread
1   green onion, chopped
$1/4$ lb (115 g) cabbage
$1/4$ cup shredded carrot
1T raisins
Salad dressing:
$1/2$ t curry powder
$1/8$ t crushed red pepper (cayenne)
$1/8$ t dill weed
$1/2$ cup plain yogurt
A pinch of salt
Barbecued chicken meat* (see below)
$1/4$ cup alfalfa sprouts
mayonnaise or butter (optional)

1. Shred cabbage. Slice barbecued chicken into thin strips. Chop carrots and set aside.

2. Mix chopped green onion and raisins, mix all salad dressing ingredients.

3. Toss with vegetables. Add dressing mixture.

4. Spread mayonnaise or butter on a slice of bread; top with vegetable mixture.

5. Top with sliced chicken and alfalfa sprouts and serve.

Barbecued chicken:

INGREDIENTS: Makes $2^1/2$ to 3 pounds (1$^1/3$ to 1 kg)
broiler-fryer cut-up chicken
Teriyaki marinade sauce:
4T soy sauce
1-in square fresh ginger root, grated
1T sake or mirin
1   clove garlic, crushed
1T honey
1. Marinate chicken pieces in the sauce for 1 hour or longer.
2. Bake chicken pieces in oven at 375°F (190°C) for 45 minutes or until tender. Baste a few times with remaining marinade sauce. For gennine BBQ flavor, barbecue chicken over charcoal fire.

SPICY SHRIMP & CUCUMBER

This enchanting combination of prawns and vegetables can be served as a light lunch.

INGREDIENTS: Serves 2

2   slices sour dough bread
2T sandwich spread
2T butter or margarine
4   prawns or $\frac{1}{4}$ lb (115 g) cocktail shrimp, cooked
$\frac{1}{4}$ cup cucumber, chopped
1T celery, chopped
1t sunflower seeds
4 to 5 drops Tabasco sauce
1   slice Swiss cheese, shredded

1. Skewer prawns as shown to prevent curling during cooking. Cook skewered prawns in lightly salted boiling water for 3 to 4 minutes.

2. Remove skewer; shell prawns and chop into small pieces.

3. Prepare cucumber and celery.

4. Mix cucumber, celery and sunflower seeds. Set aside.

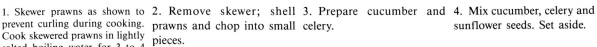

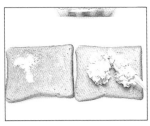

5. Mix 4 to 5 drops Tabasco sauce with sandwich spread.

6. Mix chopped prawns with vegetable mixture.

7. Add sandwich spread sauce to prawn mixture; mix well.

8. Toast and butter bread. Place prawn mixture onto toast. Top with shredded cheese and alfalfa sprouts.

TERIYAKI CHICKEN CALIFORNIA STYLE

Papaya can be used instead of avocado.

OPEN-FACE SANDWICH

INGREDIENTS: Serves 1

1 slice wheat bread
4 oz (115 g) chicken breast,
   deboned, skinned
2T *Teriyaki* sauce (see page 96)
1T vegetable oil
1 slice Provolone cheese
2 slices avocado
1T alfalfa sprouts
Light Yogurt Dressing:
1T yogurt
1/2t lemon juice
1/4t dill spice

1. Cut chicken into thin slices. Marinate chicken with *Teriyaki* sauce for 2 minutes.

2. Heat 1T oil in skillet; cook chicken until done. Set aside.

3. Place slice of cheese on chicken. Turn off heat.

4. Toast bread lightly; coat with yogurt dressing.

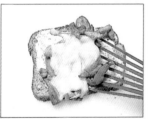  

5. Place chicken and cheese on bread.

6. Cut avocado into thin slice.

7. Top with avocado slices and alfalfa sprouts.

あたたかいうちに
どうぞ

64

SLOPPY JOE

Sloppy Joes are fun to prepare when served as a "help yourself" dish.

INGREDIENTS: Serves 2

1   hamburger bun
1T butter or margarine
8oz (225g) lean ground beef
1/2T vegetable oil
1/2 can (15oz, 425g) chili with beans
2   onions, chopped
2T ketchup
1 to 2 drops Tabasco sauce (optional)
1T shredded Swiss cheese

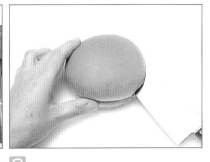

1. Heat vegetable oil in skillet over medium heat; saute chopped onion and ground beef until done. Add chili with beans; stir and mix.

2. Add 2T ketchup and mix well. Add a drop of Tabasco sauce and heat through for 3 to 5 minutes.

3. Split bun in half; toast lightly. Coat with butter. Place cooked meat onto bun. Sprinkle with shredded cheese.

TACOS

VARIATION: *Heat Taco shell and serve with chili and beans.*

To warm Taco Shells, place shells on baking sheet and heat in 350°F (175°C) pre-heated oven for 4–5 minutes until shells are crisp. Or, microwave unwrapped shells for 1–1½ minutes on high setting.

OPEN-FACE TURKEY SANDWICH

This simple sandwich can be prepared in minutes.

INGREDIENTS: Serves 2

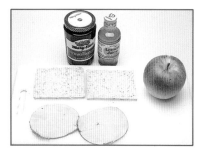

2　slices wheat bread
2　slices turkey
4　slices apple
1T lemon juice
2T strawberry jam

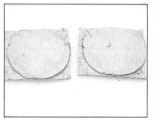

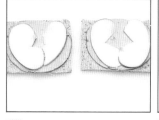

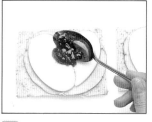

1. Place one turkey slice on each slice of bread.

2. Dip apple slices into lemon juice to prevent discoloration.

3. Place over turkey slice.

4. Top with strawberry jam.

PEACH MELBA

Serve as snack or dessert.

INGREDIENTS: Serves 1

1   slices bread
1   canned peach in syrup
1T butter or margarine
Pancake syrup or honey
Dash of cinnamon powder

1. Slice peach into small serving pieces.

2. Spread butter onto bread; arrange sliced peach onto bread. Heat in an toaster oven for 2 to 3 minutes; sprinkle with cinnamon powder and serve with syrup of your choice.

CINNAMON BAGEL

This light, quick bagel can be served at the end of an evening meal or as a midday snack.

INGREDIENTS: Serves 1

1   bagel
1T   butter
1t   sugar
1/8t cinnamon powder
1/8t grated lemon peel

1. Split bagel in half; coat with butter. Set aside. Mix sugar with cinnamon powder.

2. Spread sugar mixture and sprinkle with grated lemon peel on bagel. Toast lightly.

67

SMOKED OYSTER WITH CREAM CHEESE

OPEN-FACE SANDWICH

This dish is an excellent do-ahead recipe for a special occasion.

INGREDIENTS: Serves 1 to 2

1   slice dark bread
8oz (225g) smoked oyster or smoked baby clams, drained

8oz (225g) cream cheese, softened at room temperature
1T minced parsley
1T chopped almonds or walnuts

1. Chop smoked oyster into small pieces.

2. Mix chopped oyster with cream cheese.

3. Chop parsley.

4. Add parsley to oyster mixture. Spread on dark bread.

68

SMOKED OYSTER PARTY ROLL

The bright green provides a pleasant color contrast.

INGREDIENTS: Serves 2

1   brioch
16oz (450g) cream cheese, softened at room temperature.
2T minced parsley
1T chopped almonds or walnuts

1. Spread cream cheese on wax paper 8″ × 8″, 20 × 20 cm square.

2. Chop oyster into small pieces.

3. Place oysters on upper ⅓ of cream cheese.

4. Roll cheese and oysters into log.

5. Chop about 2T parsley.

6. Mix parseley with chopped almonds.

7. Roll completed cheese log in almond & parsley garnish. Roll in wax paper & chill until serving time.

8. Meanwhile, cut brioch in half. Serve with party roll.

COTTAGE CHEESE & PEACH

OPEN-FACE SANDWICH

This Low-calorie, nutritious dish can be made in minutes.

INGREDIENTS: Serves 1

1   slice raisin bread
2 to 2½T   small curd cottage cheese
1T   milk

¼t chives, chopped
2   peach halves (canned peach in syrup)
A   dash of cinnamon

1. Mix cottage cheese with milk and chopped chives.

2. Slice peach halves into thin slices. Set aside.

3. Spread cottage cheese mixture onto a slice of raisin bread.

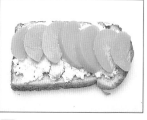

4. Top with peach slices. Sprinkle with cinnamon powder on top.

MEAT IN BREAD CUPS

Bread makes these beef cups truly unique.

1. Heat oil in skillet over medium heat; add chopped onion and saute about 3 minutes, until transparent. Add meat and cook for another 5 minutes.

2. Stir in barbecue sauce.

INGREDIENTS: Makes 6 bread cups

6 thin slices of bread
2T butter or margarine
$^1/_3$ lb (150 g) ground turkey, chicken or beef
1T chopped dry onion
1T vegetable oil
$1^1/_2$ T barbecue sauce (Teriyaki sauce)
$^1/_4$ cup shredded cheddar cheese

3. Spread butter on both sides of each slice of bread; place bread slices in muffin cups. Fill cups with cooked meat. Sprinkle shredded cheese on top. Bake in pre-heated oven at 350°F (175°C) for 5 to 7 minutes or until cheese melts.

RAISIN MUFFIN

This recipe requires only a few minutes preparation time.

1. Mix sugar with cinnamon powder.

INGREDIENTS: Serves 1

1 raisin muffin
1T butter or margarine
1t sugar

Dash of cinnamon power
12 segments of a mandarin orange, canned in syrup.

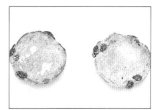

2. Split muffin in half; toast lightly and coat with butter. Sprinkle on cinnamon powder mixture. Arrange mandarin orange segments on muffin.

71

AMERICAN WEST

Petite pizza is made for an individual, single serving.

INGREDIENTS: Serves 1 to 2

1 unbaked pizza crust, pie crust, or thick slice of bread
½T olive oil
1 to 2T basic pizza sauce
2 strips bacon, cooked (see page 34)
¼ lb (115 g) lean ground beef, cooked
1T onion, chopped
¼ to ½ cup Mozzarella cheese, shredded

Basic Pizza Sauce:
makes ⅔ cup
1 8oz (225 g) canned tomato sauce
(A) ½t Italian herb seasoning mix
1⅛t crushed red pepper (cayenne)
½ clove garlic, minced
A pinch of sugar and salt

1. Mix tomato sauce with All (A) ingredients.
2. In a small sauce pan, heat tomato sauce mixture over medium heat for 20 minutes or reduce the portion to ⅔.
VARIATION: *Salsa can be used instead of (A) ingredients.*

1. On unbaked crust or thick slice of bread, coat with a layer of olive oil and pizza sauce.

2. Crumble cooked bacon.

3. Cover sauce with crumbled bacon bits or cooked hamburger.

4. Add chopped onion.

5. Top with shredded Mozzarella cheese.

6. Place in 425°F (225°C) pre-heated oven for 4-5 minutes.

Italian sausage adds a mellow flavor to this recipe.

INGREDIENTS: Makes 1 petit pizza

1   unbaked pizza crust or thick slice of bread

2–4T Basic Pizza Sauce (see page 72)

3–4 slices Italian sausage

1   green pepper, cut into thin rounds

1T green or black olives, sliced into rounds

$1/4$–$1/2$ cup shredded Mozzarella cheese

1. Prepare Basic Pizza Sauce.

2. Spoon onto bread.

3. Spread a layer of pizza sauce over the bread.

4. Cover sauce with Italian sausage slices.

5. Add sliced green pepper.

6. Add olives on top.

7. Top with shredded Mozzarella cheese.

8. Place in 425°F (225°C) pre-heated oven for 4 to 5 minutes or until cheese melts.

MEXICAN

Adding Jalapēno pepper makes this a hot dish.

INGREDIENTS: Serves 1

1 thick slice bread
2-4T basic pizza sauce (See page 72)
4 slices pepperoni
1 Jalapēno pepper, cut into thin rounds
4 mushrooms, thinly sliced
1T onion, chopped
$1/4$–$1/2$ cup Mozzarella cheese or Monterey Jack cheese, shredded

1. Spread basic pizza sauce on bread.

2. Cover sauce with pepperoni slices.

3. Add sliced Jalapēno pepper.

4. Add sliced mushrooms on top.

5. Sprinkle with chopped onion.

6. Top with shredded cheese. Bake in 425°F (225°C) pre-heated oven for 4 to 5 minutes or until cheese melts.

ALL AMERICAN

This quick and easy recipe is fun to make.

INGREDIENTS: Serves 1

1 thick slice bread
2–4T basic pizza sauce (see page 72)
2 slices ham
2T corn, cooked
1 green pepper, cut into thin rounds
1T onion, chopped
$^1/_4$–$^1/_2$ cup shredded Mozzarella cheese

1. Spread basic pizza sauce on bread.

2. Chop ham into small pieces; place over the pizza sauce.

3. Add corn.

4. Add sliced green pepper..

5. Sprinkle with chopped onion.

6. Top with cheese. Bake in 425°F (225°C) pre-heated oven for 4 to 5 minutes.

75

SILVER DELIGHT

Anchovy and cheese are a wonderful combination.

INGREDIENTS: Serves 1

1 thick slice bread
$^1/_4$–$^1/_2$ cup basic pizza sauce (see page 72)
4-5 anchovy fillets
2T chopped ham
2 black olives, sliced
1 green pepper, cut into thin rounds
1T onion, chopped
$^1/_4$–$^1/_2$ cup shredded Mozzarella cheese

1. Spread basic pizza sauce on bread; place anchovy over the sauce.

2. Add chopped ham.

3. Add sliced olives.

4. Add green pepper

5. Sprinkle with chopped onion.

6. Top with shredded cheese. Bake in pre-heated oven at 425°F (225°C) for 4 to 5 minutes or until cheese melts.

SUPER DELIGHT

This recipe is suitable for the most discriminating Italian food buff.

1. Spread basic pizza sauce on bread; Add Italian sausage.

2. Place pepperoni slices and cooked, crumbled bacon bits on top of Italian sausage.

INGREDIENTS: Serves 1

3 slices Italian sausage
3 slices pepperoni
1 strip bacon, cooked
3 mushrooms, sliced thinly
1T onion, chopped
1/2 green pepper, cut into thin slices
1T olives, chopped
1/4–1/2 cup shredded Mozzarella cheese

1 thick slice of bread
2-4T basic pizza sauce (see page 72)

3. Cover with mushroom slices.

4. Sprinkle with chopped onion.

5. Place green pepper slices on top.

6. Top with chopped olives and cheese. Bake in pre-heated oven at 425°F (225°C) for 4 to 5 minutes.

SEAFOOD DELIGHT

Serve as a light main dish accompanied by a tossed green salad.

1. Spread pizza sauce on bread; cover sauce with cocktail shrimp.

2. Place crabmeat sticks on top of shrimp.

3. Add flaked tuna fish.

4. Add green pepper.

INGREDIENTS: Serves 1

1 thick slice of bread
2-4T basic pizza sauce (see page 72)
1T cooked cocktail shrimp
3 sticks crabmeat (immitation crabmeat)
1T tuna (in a can), flaked & drained
1/2 green pepper, cut into thin slices
3 mushrooms, cut into thin slices
1/4–1/2 cup shredded Mozzarella cheese

5. Cover with mushrooms.

6. Top with shredded cheese. Bake in pre-heated oven at 425°F (225°C) for 4 to 5 minutes. 77

VEGETARIAN DELIGHT

This recipe adds a festive touch to a party brunch.

INGREDIENTS: Serves 2 to 3

1 loaf French or Hoagy bread
$^{1}/_{2}$–$^{2}/_{3}$ cup basic pizza sauce
   (See page 72)
1–2T corn, cooked
3–4 mushrooms, cut into thin
   slices
Enoki mushrooms (optional)
2 olives, cut into thin rounds
$^{1}/_{2}$ green pepper, thinly sliced
1T onion, chopped
$^{1}/_{4}$–$^{1}/_{2}$ cup shredded Mozzarella
   cheese

1 1. Cut bread in half lengthwise; spread pizza sauce on bread. cover with cooked corn.

2 2. Add mushroom slices.

3 3. Add Enoki mushrooms, if you prefer.

4 4. Place olives on top.

5 5. Add green pepper slices.

6 6. Sprinkle with chopped onion.

7 7. Top with shredded cheese; bake in 425°F (225°C) preheated oven for 4 to 5 minutes or until cheese melts.

SWEET & SOUR PORK ON A BUN

This pork recipe is enhanced with sweet-and-sour sauce.

INGREDIENTS: Serves 1

1   hamburger bun
1/4 lb (115 g) pork loin, thinly sliced
Ⓐ {
1T soy sauce
1t ginger juice
1/2t sake or cooking wine
}
1t cornstarch for dusting
1   slice pineapple ring, cut into small pieces

1T vegetable oil
Ⓑ {
1T ketchup
2T sugar
1t soy sauce
1/8t salt
2T rice vinegar
}
1t cornstarch with 1t water

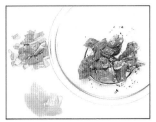

1. Marinate pork loin slices in Ⓐ sauce for 15 minutes.

2. Dust slices with cornstarch. Heat 1T oil in skillet and sauté pork until done.

3. Add chopped green pepper and pineapple chunks. Mix Ⓑ ingredients and pour into skillet. Add cornstarch & water mixture and stir until thickened.

4. Cut bun in half, toast and then add sweet sour pork.

79

NATTO SANDWICH

Natto is available at Oriental grocery stores.

INGREDIENTS: Serves 1

1 package (1³/₄ oz, 50g) *Natto*, fermented soybeans
1t soy sauce
¹/₄t mustard
1 Kaiser roll
1T butter or margarine

1. Mix natto with soy sauce and mustard.

2. Split Kaiser roll in half.

3. Toast the roll lightly; coat with butter.

4. Place natto on roll.

TOFU & TUNA SANDWICH

The use of miso is a unique characteristic of this dish.

INGREDIENTS: Serves 1 to 2

12 to 16oz (300g to 450g) firm
    tofu, well drained
2T miso (soy bean paste)
1t water
6oz (170g) tuna can, water packed
    preferred
1T onion, chopped
1T Mayonnaise
1T shredded mozzarella cheese
1 to 2T vegetable oil

* *Available at Oriental grocery stores.*

1. Pat *tofu* lightly with paper towel to remove water.

2. & 3. Cut the *tofu* into 8 slices, ¹/₂-in (1.2cm) thick.

4. Heat vegetable oil in 10-in (25cm) skillet over medium heat. Add *tofu* slices; sauté *tofu* until lightly brown on both sides. Set aside.

5. Drain tuna; mix with chopped onion and mayonnaise. Next, Mix miso with water to make a paste.

6. Spread miso onto the *tofu* pieces. Place tuna mixture on top. Sprinkle cheese on top. Broil *tofu* until cheese melts.

81

CURRY CHICKEN

Curry marinade and yogurt provide a distinctive flavor to pita bread.

INGREDIENTS: Serves 1

1   pita bread
6 oz (175 g) chicken breast, skinned, deboned
Curry Marinade:
Ⓐ
    ¼t curry powder
    ⅛t cumin
    ½T soy sauce
    1t fresh ginger root, grated
1T vegetable oil
4 oz (115 g) fresh cauliflower, cut into small pieces
1T yogurt
1t Dill weed
1 oz (30 g) tomato, diced
VARIATION: *Add shredded Swiss cheese.*

1. Cut chicken into thin strips.

2. Marinate in curry marinade sauce Ⓐ for 5 minutes.

3. Heat 1T oil in skillet over medium heat; sauté chicken strips.

4. Add cauliflower pieces; stir and cook for 3 minutes. Set aside.

5. Mix yogurt with dill weed in a small cup.

6. Split pita bread and stuff with chicken mixture.

7. Add diced tomato.

8. Spoon in yogurt and dill weed mixture.

An assortment of vegetables are stir-fried with a special sauce.

INGREDIENTS: Serves 3 to 4

2 pieces of pita bread
1 medium onion, chopped
1 cup shredded cabbage
1 small zucchini or Japanese cucumber, cut into thin rounds
1 small bunch of broccoli floret, chopped
1 small floret of cauliflower (approx. $1/8$ of a head)
1 carrot, shredded about 4oz (115g)
1-2T vegetable oil
1 clove garlic, crushed
1t basil
Salt & pepper to taste
Creamy Sauce:
Ⓐ $1/4$ cup mayonnaise
$1/4$ cup sour cream
1t lemon juice
$1/4$t pepper
$1/2$ cup shredded cheddar cheese
$1/2$ cup shredded iceberg lettuce

1. Prepare all vegetables.

2. Heat oil in skillet; sauté garlic to release aroma; add all vegetables.

3. Stir fry until the vegetables are tender but still crunchy. Season mixture with basil, salt and pepper.

4. Mix all Ⓐ ingredients together.

5. Add Ⓐ to the vegetables, tossing lightly.

6. Sprinkle shredded cheese over the warm vegetables and allow to melt.

7. Split pita bread into halves. Spoon mixture into warmed pita pockets and stuff with lettuce.

TERIYAKI STEAK SANDWICH

Today Teriyaki steak is one of the most popular dishes in the world.

INGREDIENTS: Serves 1

1 pita bread	1/4 cup onion, chopped
5oz (150g) beef (preferred cut)	1/4 cup shredded cheddar cheese
1/2 cup Teriyaki sauce (see page 96)	2T sour cream
1/2T vegetable oil	1/8t dill weed (optional)

VARIATION: *Use chicken breast instead of beef.*

1. Cut beef into medium chunks. Marinate beef chunks in *Teriyaki* sauce for 5 minutes.

2. Heat oil in skillet over medium heat; cook beef with sauce. Add chopped onions at halfway cooking point.

3. Remove from heat and pour off excess fluids. Split pita bread in half. Stuff pita pocket with beef and onion mixture.

4. Add shredded cheese. Heat in microwave oven on high for 45 seconds until cheese melts. Stuff with shredded lettuce. Mix sour cream and dill weed; pour dressing into pocket.

MACARONI & TUNA IN PITA BREAD

When you make a macaroni casserole, save leftovers for sandwiches.

INGREDIENTS: Serves 2

1 pita bread	1T chopped carrot
1 cup cooked macaroni	2T cucumber, thinly sliced
1/2 cup milk	3 radishes
Salt & pepper to taste	1t mustard
1T mayonnaise (optional)	Dash of pepper
1 can 6 1/8 oz (200 g) tuna, drained	

VARIATION: *Toast pita bread if you prefer.*
Ready made macaroni & cheese can be used.

1. Cook macaroni according to package directions. Let cool. Add milk, salt & pepper and mix well. Add chopped carrot and sliced cucumber.

2. Cut radishes into thin rounds; add to macaroni mixture.

3. Add flaked tuna into macaroni mixture and stir well.

4. Cut pita bread in half; stuff with macaroni mixture.

TUNA IN POCKET BREAD

There are many ways to prepare and serve tuna fish. This is one colorful and easy way to make a sandwich.

INGREDIENTS: Makes 2 pita pockets

1	piece of pita bread
1/2	carrot, shredded
1/4	cup celery, chopped
1/2	cup lettuce, shredded
1/2	apple, cored, finely chopped
1/8t	lemon juice
1	can 6 1/2 to 7 oz (200 g to 210 g) tuna, drained
1/2	cup shredded lettuce for topping

Salad Dressing:
2T mayonnaise
1t Dijon mustard
1t poppy seeds (optional)

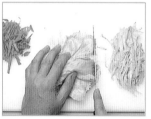   

1. Prepare all vegetables. Sprinkle lemon juice over chopped apple to prevent discoloration.

2. Cut pita in half; toast lightly.

3. Mix vegetables and tuna.

4. Add chopped apple.

5. Mix mayonnaise, mustard and poppy seeds together.

6. Add to tuna mixture.

7. Stuff pita with mixture.

8. Top with shredded lettuce

STIR-FRIED CHICKEN IN PITA BREAD

Warm pita bread on ungreased cookie sheet in pre-heated oven at 350°F (175°C) for 3 minutes.

INGREDIENTS: Makes 2 pita pockets

1 piece of pita bread
1/4 carrot, match-stick thin strips
1/4 lb (115 g) cabbage, shredded
4 large mushrooms, sliced
1/2 chicken breast, deboned, skinned
1T vegetable oil
1 clove garlic, minced
1t grated ginger root
1/8t crushed red pepper (cayenne)
1/4t curry powder
1t *sake* or cooking wine
Soy sauce and salt to taste
2 leaves lettuce

1. Prepare vegetables. Set aside.

2. Cut chicken breast into thin strips.

3. Heat oil in skillet over medium heat; stir fry garlic, ginger root and chicken strips until chicken is done.

4. Add red pepper, curry powder, *sake*, soy sauce and salt to taste.

5. Add carrot, cabbage and mushrooms; stir fry for a few minutes or until vegetables are tender.

6. Cut pita bread in half; toast lightly. Stuff pockets with 1 leaf lettuce each and the cooked chicken mixture. 87

PARTY SCENE

INFORMATION

HELPFUL HINTS

BREADS

Fresh breads whose fragrant aromas have always delighted us and stimulate appetite. It is not difficult to make your own bread at home, however varieties of breads are readily available today.

The basic ingredients for yeast breads:

Yeast: Yeast which comes in two forms, active dry granule or fresh cake yeast.

Flour: A different kind of bread depends on proportion and type of flour you use. There are whole-wheat, buckwheat all-purpose, soy, rice, rye, corn, oatmeal, potato four and unprocessed bran.

Liquid: Water, milk or a combination of the two are used for breads.

Sugar: A little sugar or molasses is used for flavor.

Salt: Salt also enhances flavor.

Fat: Butter, margarine, salad oil, shortening or lard can be used making the breads.

Fgg: Eggs add flavor for breads.

Other ingredients: Nuts, seeds, fruit, herbs, vegetables and wheat germ can be added to a yeast dough.

STORING BREAD

Wrap in plastic wrap or foil and seal tightly to keep bread fresh.

Bread may be stored in the freezer no more than one year. To thaw unsliced bread, let stand, wrapped for a crisp crust, at room temperature for 2 to 3 hours. Frozen slices of bread can be popped into the toaster without thawing.

To restore the fresh-baked flavor of bread, wrap bread in foil and reheat in a 375°F oven about 20 minutes.

Day-old-bread can be used for different recipes.

1. Bread crumbs; Place bread slices on a cookie sheet; reheat in a 400°F oven about 6 to 10 minutes. Place in a paper or plastic bag and press over with a pastry roller.

2. Bread sticks: Cut bread slices into thick matchsticks. Deep fry until golden; sprinkle with cinnamon powder and sugar mixture. Or bake in a 400°F oven for 5 to 7 minutes until golden. Pour some melted butter over bread sticks and coat with cinnamon and sugar mixture.

3. Croutons: Cut bread slices into ½-inch cubes. Heat butter or salad oil in skillet over medium heat; add one small garlic clove and cook until golden. Discard garlic and add bread cubes and minced parsley; cook with a stir-fry motion, until the cubes are crisp and golden. For stuffing, add herbs of your choice.

HELPFUL HINTS

BREADS	FLOUR
WHITE	ALL-PURPOSE
WHOLE-WHEAT	WHOLE-WHEAT, ALL-PURPOSE
RYE	ALL-PURPOSE, RYE,
WHOLE-GRAIN	RYE, UNPROCESSED BRAN, WHEAT GERM, WHOLE-WHEAT, CORNMEAL
PUMPERNICKEL	ALL-PURPOSE, RYE, WHOLE-WHEAT
ITALIAN	ALL-PURPOSE
FRENCH	ALL-PURPOSE, CORNMEAL
SOURDOUGH	ALL-PURPOSE
CORN	CORN, ALL-PURPOSE
POTATO	POTATO, ALL-PURPOSE
CARAWAY SEEDS	ALL-PURPOSE
RAISIN	ALL-PURPOSE
NUTS	ALL-PURPOSE
PITA (POCKET)	ALL-PURPOSE
SODA	ALL-PURPOSE
SESAME	ALL-PURPOSE
KUMMEL BROT	ALL-PURPOSE, RYE
SOUR RYE	ALL-PURPOSE, RYE
WHEAT GERM	WHOLE-WHEAT, WHEAT GERM
OATMEAL	ALL-PURPOSE, QUICK-COOKING OATS
ZUCCHINI	ALL-PURPOSE
SPINACH	ALL-PURPOSE
CRISP BREAD	ALL-PURPOSE, RYE
KNACKEBROT	WHOLE-WHEAT, RYE, BUCKWHEAT
TORTILLAS, TACO SHELLS	CORNMEAL, WHOLE-WHEAT

DINNER ROLLS	FLOUR
HARD ROLL BUNS, HAMBURGER BUNS	ALL-PURPOSE
CRESCENTS	ALL-PURPOSE
VIENNA	ALL-PURPOSE
BRIOCHES	ALL-PURPOSE
CROISSANTS	ALL-PURPOSE
BISCUITS	ALL-PURPOSE
POPOVERS	ALL-PURPOSE
SCONES	ALL-PURPOSE
BAGELS	ALL-PURPOSE
MUFFINS	ALL-PURPOSE

CHEESE

Cheese which is rich in vitamin A and calcium is among the most important ingredients for sandwich making.

Cheese falls into three types.

1. Natural cheese: Natural cheese is made from milk.
2. Process cheese: Process cheese is made from blend of one or more natural cheese and milk solids should be at least 40% or more.
3. Cheese food: Cheese food is made by blending one or more natural and process cheese and cheese contents should be 51% or more.

STORING CHEESE

All cheese should be stored in the refrigerator, tightly wrapped in foil, place in a plastic bag to prevent them from drying out.

Some cheese such as Parmigiano Reggiano should be wrapped in a thin layer of dampened cheese cloth, then plastic wrap and an outer layer of foil to prevent them from drying out, then store in the refrigerator. If some hard cheese such as cheddar cheese turns moldy on the surface, cut off the affected piece or scrap the surface clean. If the mold has penetrated the cheese, discard the cheese.

FREEZING CHEESE

To freeze cheese, wrap cheese tightly with freezer wrap to prevent them from drying out. Some soft cheese such as creamed cottage chesse is not recommended for freezing.

To thaw cheese, place in the refrigerator and thaw them slowly.

To serve cheese, remove cheese from refrigerator about one hour before serving and let it warm to room temperature. Mold-ripened cheeses, such as Roquefort or Gorgonzola which has their distinctive flavor from the mold should be placed on a board or plate and cover with a glass bowl.

Leftover cheese which is too dry or hard to eat should be grated or cut into chunks for cooking and garnishing.

COUNTRY	CHEESE	FLAVOR-TYPE	USE
DENMARK	BLEU	MOLD-RIPPENED	SANDWICHES, SALADS, SNACKS, DESSERT
ENGLAND	CHEDDAR	FIRM, MILD TO EXTRA SHARP	SANDWICHES, SNACKS, DESSERT, COOKING
	CHESHIRE	FIRM, MILD TO SHARP	COOKING, SNACKS
	STILTON	MOLD-RIPENED	SNACKS, SALADS, DESSERT
FRANCE	FROMAGE FRAIS	SOFT	SANDWICHES, APPETIZERS, DESSERT
	ROQUEFORT	MOLD-RIPENED	APPETIZERS, SNACKS, SANDWICHES, SALADS, COOKING
	PORT DU SALUT	SEMI-SOFT	SNACK, SANDWICHES, DESSERT
	MUENSTER	SEMI-SOFT	APPETIZERS, SANDWICHES, SNACKS
	CHEVRETINES	SEMI-SOFT	APPETIZERS, SNACKS
	GAPERON	SEMI-SOFT	COOKING, SNACKS
	VALENCAY	MOLD-RIPENED	APPETIZERS, SNACKS
	EPOISSES	SOFT, MILD	APPETIZERS, SNACKS
	DELICE DE SALIGNY	SEMI-SOFT	APPETIZERS, SNACKS
	LE ROC-AMADOUR	SEMI-SOFT	SNACKS, DESSERT

HELPFUL HINTS

COUNTRY	CHEESE	FLAVOR-TYPE	USE
FRANCE	REBLOCHON	SEMI-SOFT	APPETIZERS, SNACKS, DESSERT
	BANON	SEMI-SOFT	APPETIZERS, SNACKS, DESSERT
	RACLETTE	SOFT	COOKING, APPETIZERS
	COULOMMIERS	SOFT	APPETIZERS, SNACKS, DESSERT
	SELLES SUV CHEV	SOFT, RIPPENED	APPETIZERS, SNACKS, DESSERT
	CAMEMBERT	SOFT	APPETIZERS, SNACKS, DESSERT
GREEK	FETA	SEMI-SOFT	APPETIZERS, SALADS, SNACKS, COOKING
GERMANY	MUENSTER	SEMI-SOFT	SANDWICHES, SNACKS, DESSERT
	LIMBURGER	SOFT	SANDWICHES, SNACKS, APPETIZERS, DESSERT
HOLLAND	EDAM, GOUDA	FIRM	SNACKS, DESSERT, SANDWICHES, COOKING
ITALY	MAIALINO	SEMI-SOFT	SNACKS
	FONTINA	FIRM	SNACKS, DESSERT, COOKING
	FONTIELLA	FIRM	SNACKS, DESSERT, COOKING
	GORGONZOLA	MOLD-RIPENED	SALADS, DESSERT
	MOZZARELLA	SEMI-SOFT	COOKING, SNACKS
	PARMINGIANO REGGIANO	HARD	COOKING
	PECORINO ROMANO	HARD	COOKING
	PROVOLONE	FIRM	COOKING, SNACKS
	RICOTTA SALATA	SEMI-SOFT	COOKING, SNACKS
	SARDO	FIRM	COOKING, DESSERT
	PARMESAN	HARD	COOKING
NORWAY	GJETÖST	FIRM	SANDWICHES, SNACKS
SWITZERLAND	SWISS (EMMENTHALER)	FIRM	APPETIZERS, SANDWICHES, COOKING
	GRUYERE	FIRM	COOKING, DESSERT, SNACKS
	RACLETTE	SEMI-FIRM	SNACKS, COOKING
U.S.A.	CHEDDAR	HARD	APPETIZERS, SNACKS, COOKING, SANDWICHES
	MONTEREY JACK	SEMI-SOFT	APPETIZERS, SNACKS, SANDWICHES, COOKING
	NEUFCHÂTEL	SOFT	COOKING, SANDWICHES, SALADS, APPETIZERS
	SWISS	FIRM	COOKING, SANDWICHES, SNACKS, APPETIZERS
	BLUE	SEMI-SOFT	APPETIZERS, COOKING, SALADS, SANDWICHES
	BRICK	SEMI-SOFT	APPETIZERS, SANDWICHES, SNACKS
	COTTAGE CHEESE	SOFT	SALADS, SANDWICHES, SNACKS, COOKING
	CREAM CHEESE	SOFT	APPETIZERS, SANDWICHES, CAKES

TIPS FOR SANDWICH MAKING

Preparation:

1. Read recipes carefully and thoroughly.
2. Write down all necessary ingredients you need to buy.
3. Arrange all necessary seasonings, spices, herbs, butter, margarine, sandwich spreads, condiments, and breads on kitchen counter or within your reach.
4. Check all cooking equipment and place within reach.
5. Prepare measuring cups, spoons and knives.
6. Place all serving bowls, plates, sandwich bags, plastic wrap and foil with in reach.
7. Consider the number of sandwiches you want to make and whether you will serve sandwiches for lunches, snackes, picnics or etc.

Basic Cutting Methods:

Various cutting methods make cooking time short, and appearance attractive.

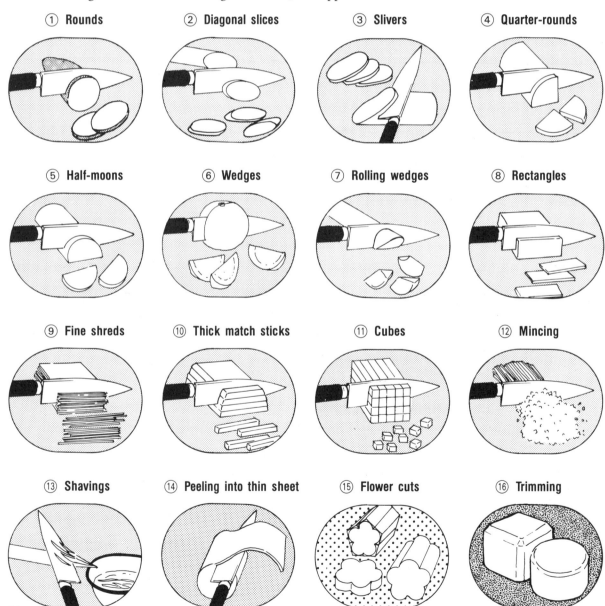

① **Rounds** ② **Diagonal slices** ③ **Slivers** ④ **Quarter-rounds**

⑤ **Half-moons** ⑥ **Wedges** ⑦ **Rolling wedges** ⑧ **Rectangles**

⑨ **Fine shreds** ⑩ **Thick match sticks** ⑪ **Cubes** ⑫ **Mincing**

⑬ **Shavings** ⑭ **Peeling into thin sheet** ⑮ **Flower cuts** ⑯ **Trimming**

TIPS FOR SANDWICH MAKING

Decorative Cutting methods:

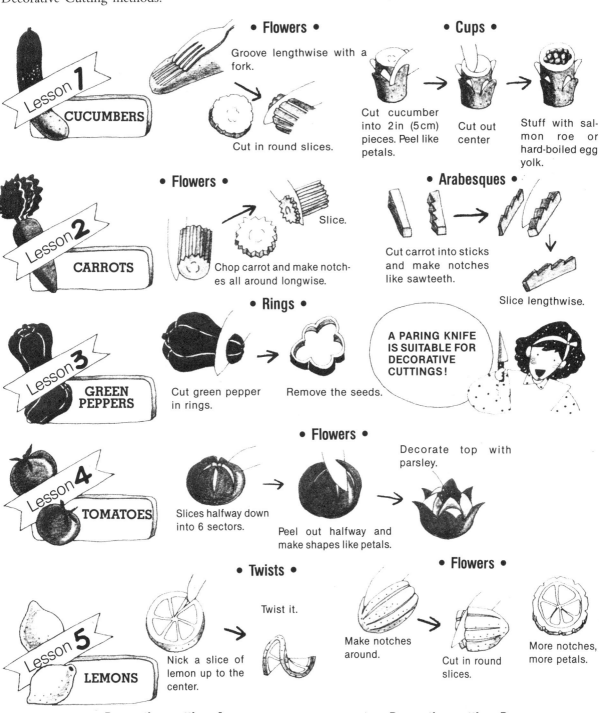

Lesson 1 — CUCUMBERS

• Flowers •
Groove lengthwise with a fork.
Cut in round slices.

• Cups •
Cut cucumber into 2in (5cm) pieces. Peel like petals.
Cut out center
Stuff with salmon roe or hard-boiled egg yolk.

Lesson 2 — CARROTS

• Flowers •
Chop carrot and make notches all around longwise.
Slice.

• Arabesques •
Cut carrot into sticks and make notches like sawteeth.
Slice lengthwise.

Lesson 3 — GREEN PEPPERS

• Rings •
Cut green pepper in rings.
Remove the seeds.

A PARING KNIFE IS SUITABLE FOR DECORATIVE CUTTINGS!

Lesson 4 — TOMATOES

• Flowers •
Slices halfway down into 6 sectors.
Peel out halfway and make shapes like petals.
Decorate top with parsley.

Lesson 5 — LEMONS

• Twists •
Nick a slice of lemon up to the center.
Twist it.

• Flowers •
Make notches around.
Cut in round slices.
More notches, more petals.

• Decorative cutting A •

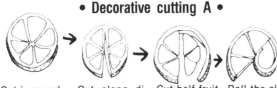

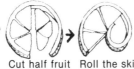

Cut in round slices.
Cut along diameter almost to the end.
Cut half fruit off the skin.
Roll the skin inside.

• Decorative cutting B •

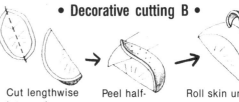

Cut lengthwise into wedges.
Peel halfway.
Roll skin under.

TIPS FOR SANDWICH MAKING

To make large quantities, line up the bread slices in row, two by two, and coat them with butter or sandwich spread of your choice. Spread the filling on one row; top with remaining slices; cut and wrap sandwiches. For lunches or picnics, wrap tomato or lettuce separately, so bread will not get soggy. Many sandwiches can be frozen up to 2 weeks before serving. Sandwiches can be enjoyed all year round, so try them whenever you like.

SANDWICH SPREAD:

Butter & mustard
Butter & crushed garlic
Butter & minced parsley
Butter & curry powder
Mayonnaise & minced parsley
Mayonnaise & wasabi paste
Mayonnaise & mustard
Mayonnaise & soy sauce

Mayonnaise & curry powder
Mayonnaise & Parmesan cheese
Mayonnaise & chili sauce & ketchup
Cottage cheese & chives
Cottage cheese & pineapple chuncks
Cream cheese & Parmesan cheese
Peanut butter & jam
Chicken, pork or beef liver wurst

GARNISHES:

Potato chips······plain, sour cream & onion, beef
                    consomme, onion, garlic
Nacho cheese
Corn chips, Tortilla chips
Sweet & dill pickles

Black and green olives
Fruits and vegetables
Salads
Fresh fruits······apple, banana, grapes, grapefruits,
                    orange, pear, watermelon, melon canta-
                    ropes, purune, prum, cherry, pineapple
                    and other fruits.

BEVERAGES:
Coffe, tea, milk, cocoa, chocolate, lemonade, soda, shakes, cola, pepsi, 7-up, other soft drinks, fruit juice of your choice.

ADDITIONAL SPECIAL SANDWICHES·RECIPES

TOFU OPEN-FACED SANDWICH

2 servings

14—16 oz (300—450 g) firm *tofu*, well drained
1T vegetable oil
2T salsa
2T shredded mozzarella cheese

1. Heat oil in skillet over medium heat.
2. Cut *tofu* into fourths crosswise.
3. Grill *tofu* on both sides until light brown.
4. Place *tofu* pieces on a cookie sheet; spoon salsa on *tofu*.
5. Add shredded cheese on top.
6. Broil until cheese melts.

MISO CHICKEN SANDWICH

1 serving
1 English muffin, split open
$2^1/_2$—4 oz (75—115 g) thinly sliced breast of chicken

1T miso sauce*	*Miso sauce:
1T vegetable oil	1T red miso
1T mayonnaise	$^1/_2$T mirin
1 leaf lettuce	$^1/_2$t. sugar
2 slices tomato	$^1/_2$t sake
	$^1/_8$t sesame seeds

1. Marinate chicken in miso sauce for 5 minutes.
2. Heat oil in skillet over medium heat; sauté chicken for 5 minutes. Set aside.
3. Toast English muffin; coat with mayonnaise.
4. Put on lettuce.
5. Place chicken on lettuce leaf.
6. Top off with tomato slices.

VARIATION: Use favorite BBQ sauce instead of miso sauce. Add slice of Swiss cheese.

OPEN-FACED VEGETABLE-CHEESY

2 servings

2 cheese English muffins, split open	$^1/_2$t. basil
	1t. oregano
1 cup button mushrooms, sliced	1T vegetable oil
	1T butter or margarine
$^1/_2$ cup bean sprouts	Salt & pepper to taste
$^1/_2$ cup yellow squash or eggplant, sliced	$^1/_2$ cup shredded Gouda or cheddar cheese
1 clove garlic, minced	

1. Heat vegatable oil in skillet over medium heat; stir fry mushrooms, bean sprouts, squash and garlic.
2. Stir in basil, oregano, salt and pepper while cooking.
3. Toast English muffins lightly and butter them.
4. Top muffins with cooked vegetable mixture, then shredded cheese.
5. Broil until cheese melts, about 4 to 5 minutes.

TERIYAKI BURGER

1 serving

1 hamburger bun, split open	1 clove garlic, crushed
	$^1/_2$t sake or cooking wine
$^1/_4$lb (115 g) ground beef	$^1/_4$t mirin (Japanese sweet cooking wine)
Teriyaki Sauce:	
1T soy sauce	$^1/_8$t sugar
$^1/_2$t grated fresh ginger root	1T mayonnaise

1. Mix ground beef with Teriyaki sauce.
2. Make patti.
3. Grill or broil hamburger patti until done.
4. Toast hamburger bun.
5. Spread mayonnaise.
6. Place patti on the bun.

VARIATION: Add lettuce and tomato slices if you desire.

GLOSSARY: INGREDIENTS

BASIL (SWEET)······A fresh, sweet basil with dark green leaves with a purple stem. The flavor is like aromatic licorice. Fresh mint can be an acceptable substitute in cooking.

BEAN SPROUTS······The sprouts of the mung beans. Use fresh sprouts if possible. Store bean sprouts in fresh water and store in the refrigerator.

CAYENNE PEPPER······Cayenne pepper is commonly called chilies or red pepper which is the ground product of the dried ripe fruit of several different species of small fruited Capsicum plants.

CHILIES······The small green chilies are the most popular chilies used in cooking. These chilies are very hot and the amount used in each recipe is determined by individual preference. Chilies can be made less hot by removing the seeds.

CUCUMBERS······American cucumbers are equivalent to 2 to 3 Japanese cucumbers. In general, peel and seed cucumbers unless skin is delicate and thin and seeds are immature. If using the small Japanese variety, it is not necessary to peel or seed.

CUMIN······An essential spice powder used in the making of some dishes such as curries. If using seeds, roasting before grinding imparts a fuller flavor.

CURRY POWDER······A blend of many different spices.

EGGPLANTS······Size varies with region and season, 2-oz (60 g) to approximately 10-oz (285 g) each.

GARLIC······A main ingredient for many foods. Use fresh garlic for best flavor.

GINGER ROOT······A rhizome of the ginger plant. Young ginger has a very translucent skin. The mature ginger has a brown skin which should be peeled before using. Fresh ginger root imparts hotness and flavor to the food.

MINT LEAVES······The fresh leaves of mint. Used in recipes to impart refreshing aroma.

MIRIN······*Mirin* is called sweet cooking rice wine and used for cooking.

MISO······*Miso* is fermented soybean paste. The colors range from yellow to brown; yellow *miso* is referred to as shiro *miso* and brown *miso* is called *aka miso*. It is used for soup, dressing, sauces, etc.

MUSHROOMS······Fresh button mushrooms are most often found in grocery stores. Slice or use whole as indicated in recipes. Black-dried mushrooms should be soaked in warm water to soften. Rinse and then use in recipes as required. Keeps indefinitely on shelf.

NATTO······This is a fermented soybean preparation made by the action of special bacteria. It has a rich cheese-like flavor with a sticky consistency.

OREGANO······Use oregano sparingly because of the herb's strong, spicy flavor. The best quality comes from Italy, Greece and Mexico. Oregano holds its flavor for long period in storage.

SAKE······*Sake* is made by inoculating steamed mold and then allowing fermentation to occur. It is then refined. In Japan, *sake* is the most popular beverage, but it is also used in various ways in cooking.

SESAME SEEDS······Both black and white sesame seeds are available. When toasted, sesame seeds have a much richer flavor.

SHISO **LEAVES**······These minty, aromatic leaves come in green and red varieties.

SOYBEANS······Soybeans were one of the five sacred grains of ancient China. They have many cultivars including black and yellow ones and countless uses: They can be used in stew, turned into soy paste, soy milk, also *tofu*, and can be used as a meat substitute.

SOY SAUCE······Soy sauce is made from soybeans and salt. It is the primary seasoning in Japanese cooking and now is considered an International seasoning. It is used for simmered foods, dressings, soups, sauces and etc.
Ordinary soy sauce is dark and a light color is also available. The light soy sauce does not darken the colors of food, and it is salty enough. It is also low-salt soy sauce which is available at the grocery stores.

TOFU······*Tofu*, "bean curd" in English, is an important product of soy beans. It is rich in protein, vitamins and minerals. It is low in calories and saturated fats, and entirely free of cholesterol. There are two kinds of *tofu: Firm* and *soft tofu*.

WASABI······*Wasabi* is Japanese horseradish. It is pale green in color. It has a more delicate aroma and is milder tasting than western horseradish. Usually it comes in a powdered form or in tube. The powder should be mixed with water to make a thick paste.

GLOSSARY: INGREDIENTS

MEAT & MEAT PRODUCTS

BEEF TONGUE

CORNED BEEF

CANADIAN BACON

PORK

LIVERWURST

PASTRAMI

SALAMI

SAUSAGE

TERRINE

(garlic, ginger, onion, spinach, mush-rooms, *shiso* leaves)

(fish, poultry or meat pate are cooked in a dish)

GLOSSARY: INGREDIENTS

GROUND TURKEY

TURKEY, UNSLICED

TURKEY SLICES

SEAFOOD

ANCHOVY FILLETS

IMMITATION CRABMEAT

PREPARED COD FISH ROE

SMOKED OYSTER

SMOKED SALMON

CRABMEAT

GLOSSARY: INGREDIENTS

MAYONNAISE & PICKLES

REGULAR MAYONNAISE

LOW-FAT MAYONNAISE

SANDWICH SPREAD

BLUE CHEESE DRESSING

DILL PICKLES

SWEET PICKLES

BLACK OLIVES, SLICED

HORSERADISH

MUSTARD WITH HORSE RADISH

GLOSSARY: INGREDIENTS

CANNED FOODS, JAM, PEANUT BUTTER

ARTICHOKE HEATS INSTANT

SAUERKRAUT IN A CAN

PORK & BEANS

CHILI WITH BEANS

STRAWBERRY JAM GRAPE JAM

CHUNKY PEANUT BUTTER

DILL WEED

MRS. DASH

SALSA

The flavor of dill is somewhat pungent, and the stems have a bitterness that almost burns. Yet as a seasoning in sweet and bland vegetables it has a most pleasing taste and exceedingly effective flavor.

(salt substitute)—An all natural blend of 14 herbs and spices and other seasonings are mixed together to give flavor to food insted of salt.
JALOPENÁ PEPPER & green chili pepper-Use peppers after removing seeds.

(TOMATO, LEMON, GARIC, CILANTRO, GREEN ONION, PEPPERS)

EQUIPMENT

Very few pieces of equipment are required for the making of sandwiches. Most kitchens of today are supplied with the essentials such as knives, forks, a cutting board, pots and pans, skillets and other cooking utensils. However, some of the following equipment and utensils may help you and you may find it a pleasure cooking with them.

BAMBOO SKEWERS

Bamboo skewers are a very handy tool. They are not only used for many grilled dishes, but to test foods for doneness by pricking and also for cooking raw shrimp to prevent curling while boiling.

A BLENDER OR FOOD PROCESSOR

Chopping, mixing and other tsks can be done easily.

GARLIC PRESS

Used to crush garlic cloves.

MICROWAVE OVEN

For cooking foods speedily and cleanly. Without heating the utensils or oven, only the foods are heated. The food must contain some moisture, and metal container or china with metal decorations are not suitable (metal cause sparks). Microwave do a good job in thawing meats or fish and reheating foods.

NON-STICK SKILLET

It is made of rustproof aluminum. Precondition by rubbing in small amount of salad oil on surface.

ONION CHOPPER

This tool is useful for chopping onion or nuts into small pieces.

PLASTIC BAGS

Different sizes are available to seals in freshness.

TOASTER

4-slice toasters with dual control can be handy for toasting bread slices and some frozen pastries at the same time.

WOK

There are round-bottomed and flat-bottomed, or one-handled and two-handled types. For home use, round bottomed ones with side handles are recommended. Materials should be cast-iron since stainless scorches easily and Teflon-coats are easily scarred. Cast-iron woks are multi-purpose pots; stir-frying, deep-frying, simmering and steaming with bamboo steamer.

INDEX

INDEX